SEXUAL PALMISTRY

Integrating scientific hand analysis with contemporary insights
into the psychology of sexuality.

SEXUAL PALMISTRY

Hand Analysis Techniques
——— for dealing with ———
Love, Sex and Relationships

by

NATHANIEL ALTMAN

Illustrated by Linda James

THE AQUARIAN PRESS
Wellingborough, Northamptonshire

First published July 1986
Second Impression August 1986

British Library Cataloguing in Publication Data

Altman, Nathaniel
  Sexual palmistry: hand analysis techniques for
  dealing with love, sex and relationships
  1. Palmistry and sex
  I. Title II. James, Linda
  133.6   BF935.S4

ISBN 0-85030-455-5

The Aquarian Press is part of the Thorsons Publishing Group

Printed and bound in Great Britain

CONTENTS

Acknowledgements
The author would like to thank the following people
who helped in the preparation of this book; José
Alberto Rosa, M.D., Sadie Davis Altman, Gregory
Leo, Peter Massey, Terri Raymond, Wayne Perez,
Robert G. Lee.

PREFACE

Perhaps the most deeply felt dissatisfaction in our culture is the ungroundedness of our sexual lives and the difficulty in establishing deep and satisfying romantic relationships with others. Although we have more material knowledge about the philosophy of sex and sexual technique than ever before in history, many of us are ignorant of our overall psychosexual make-up and are not in touch with our own affectional and sexual needs.

When we come in to the world we arrive with definite character traits which will eventually mould our psychosexual personality. And from the time we are born, we are given our sexual education. From our parents we learn about trust, caring and unconditional love. Sometimes we learn about cruelty, withholding and betrayal. In addition to learning how to read and write, our schooling often reinforces our earliest attitudes, or teaches us new ones. Those of us who received a traditional religious education may have early memories about sexual teaching which we are not likely to forget.

The media has also played an important role in our sexual education, as well as the way we view relationships. Years ago, radio, television and magazines promoted what are now called 'traditional family values'. Sex was taught to be something apart from the rest of one's life. Men were taught to be dominant, 'macho' and independent, while women were portrayed as submissive, compliant and dependent on men. At the same time that woman was idealized as a cross between an asexual saint and a 'good little housewife and mother', she was also portrayed as little more than a common harlot in men's magazines. It is little wonder that both men and women have been in conflict about sex roles today and that relationships often resemble a union of enemies rather than one of close friends.

During the 'sexual revolution' which began in the 1960s, many of these images and repressive patterns began to dissolve. In the quest for sexual liberation, we have now more access to sexual information than ever before. In movies, books and magazines, explicit sex has become so commonplace that it is now considered routine. We are constantly bombarded with sexual come-ons in advertising – from shampoo to automobiles – to the extent that sex has become almost totally depersonalized. People become sexual objects to be used and discarded. All this pressure does, unfortunately, have an impact on our relationships. In large cities especially, it is difficult for two people to really get to know each other and to establish the deep foundations necessary for achieving an enduring and satisfying relationship.

Of course, there is a side of the human personality which 'hooks in' to depersonalized sex and disposable relationships. We like the variety and excitement they bring, and enjoy the freedom from breaking with old, repressive and often hypocritical sexual standards. However, for many, the growing sense of depersonalization – both sexual and other-wise – is a source of frustration and loneliness, especially among those who live in large cities.

On the other side, there is a part of us which yearns for closeness, deep contact and commitment in our relationships with others. This is the side of us which yearns for supportive friendship and wants our sexual feelings to be channelled towards achieving greater intimacy and caring.

Relationships are essential for both spiritual progress and psychological well-being. While we all need and deserve time by ourselves, the quality and depth of our relationships with others (whether romantic or not) is a mirror of our own state of being and thus can be a reliable guide to our degree of personal integration and self-fulfilment.

Although learning to understand oneself and others sexually is important, we also need to see people in their totality, rather than primarily in a sexual context. We need to know them as people with an understanding and appreciation of their character, mind, special talents, aspirations and ability to love.

Like modern astrology, numerology and handwriting analysis, the art and science of palmistry enables us to know ourselves and others better. Through a systematic study of hand shape, hand motility, skin texture, hand elevations and lines, we can achieve a deeper understanding of our essential instincts and personality traits, and how they are expressed in daily life and especially in our relationships with others.

Very few books have been written about sexual palmistry. Those which have been published have either contained strong moral overtones about relationship and sexuality, or tend to trivialize sex and refuse to discuss aspects of sexuality which are controversial or psychologically uncomfortable. Others concentrate on how you can 'catch' your ideal mate by a study of his/her hands.

While this book may not have all the answers, it is the author's hope that it will instead lead the reader to go more deeply into all aspects of sexuality and relationship as they pertain to palmistry, so that a broader and deeper level of self-understanding can be achieved. At the same time, it is hoped that for those who wish to read the hands of others, this increased understanding of the essence of sexual palmistry will enable the palmist to better counsel others so that they can reach their full potential as loving human beings.

Nathaniel Altman
Brooklyn, New York

SECTION I: GROUNDING

This section provides a basis upon which we can begin to interpret the individual fingers, mounts, lines and other aspects of the hand in terms of sexual nature.

Chapter 1
THE FOUNDATIONS OF SEXUAL PALMISTRY

The hand has fascinated us since the beginning of human history. Recorded studies of the human hand – both as a tool for creative expression and as a reflection of our inner selves – go back over 5,000 years. It is believed that the ancient Chinese began studying the form, lines and colour of the hand as early as 3000 BC, and called their science *siang cheou*.

In India years later, Aryan sages developed the study of hand analysis, *hast samudrika shastra*, as part of a larger science (samudrika shastra) which interprets and forecasts human nature and destiny by examining the forehead, face, hands, chest and feet.

Although no written records remain, it is known that the ancient Chaldeans, Tibetans, Sumerians and Babylonians studied the science of hand analysis, as well as the early Hebrews, Egyptians and Persians. Throughout the Middle East today, hand reading, known as *ilm-ul-kaff* is a highly respected study and avocation.

The Greeks were also enthusiastic students of hand symbology and hand analysis, and coined the term *chirosophy* (from *xier*, hand and *sophia*, wisdom). Aristotle is credited with having written several specialized treatises on hands, including one written especially for Alexander the Great. He was particularly interested in the markings of the hand and the significance they have in our lives. In *De coelo et mundi causa* he wrote 'The lines are not written into the human hand without reason; they come from heavenly influences and man's own individuality.' In addition to Aristotle and Alexander, Claudius Galen, Anaxagoras, Hippocrates, Artemodoros of Ephesus and Claudius Ptolemaeus were serious students of medical and psychological chirosophy as well as *chiromancy*, the art of foretelling the future by the lines in the hand.

When people consult a hand reader, they are mainly interested in chiromancy. They want to know how long they will live, how much money they will earn or inherit, when they will get married or divorced, and how many children they will have. Over the centuries, in fact, the primary work of most palmists has involved the telling of fortunes and offering predictions to satisfy their clients' curiosity. Since hand reading is an intuitive art as well as a science, many predictions have been found to be true. However, since the lines of the hand can change within the space of a few weeks, predictions are often inaccurate or even harmful, because they can dampen one's initiative and help us avoid taking personal responsibility for our attitudes and actions. For this reason, predictive hand analysis is used to a lesser extent than in earlier times by responsible hand readers, especially when they focus on issues involving sexuality and relationship.

As opposed to chiromancy, *chirology* should be the palmist's major concern. Chirology is primarily psychologically orientated palmistry, and is based on the idea that as both a tactile instrument and work tool, the hand possesses a unique ability to express *who we are*.

By the time we are 12–14 months old, psychologists say that our hand gestures have begun to communicate feelings of need, joy, sorrow, anger, surprise and caring. They serve as vital components in everyday speech and enable us to share our deepest feelings with others. Although our posture, manner of walking and facial expression all reveal our inner being to some extent, the hands are more expressive, more specific, and can reflect the essence of our being with greater depth and accuracy than perhaps any other part of the body. This fact impressed the noted psychiatrist Carl Jung to such a degree that he decided to study psycho-chirology himself. In the introduction he prepared for *The Hands of Children*, a pioneer psychological work by Julius Speer, Jung wrote: 'Hands, whose shape and functioning are so intimately connected with the psyche, might provide revealing, and therefore interpretable expressions of psychological peculiarity, that is, of human character.'

Why is this? As our basic instrument of touch, the hand plays a leading role in conditioning the brain, body and emotions to develop certain responses to the world around us. In addition to our inherent genetic make-up, the hands can reveal changing patterns of health, emotional stability, the unfoldment of talents, and major events which are determined by the way we respond to life experience. Since the lines of the hand can change, the hand offers us a special opportunity to monitor our life path, and see into the past, present and potential future. These areas are discussed in detail in my previous book, *The Palmistry Workbook*.

Perhaps nowhere is the hand more revealing than in the areas of sexuality and relationship. From the earliest days of life, our hands play a unique role in enabling us to relate both to the people around us and to the world at large.

As infants, we touch everything we can in an urgent quest to perceive and experience our surroundings: hands are our principal tool of tactile investigation. Because the hands are among the most sensitive parts of the body, they can receive manifold impressions of pressure, texture, temperature and spatial dynamics. According to the psychiatrist and chirologist Charlotte Wolff, Fellow of the Royal Institute of Psychiatry, 'Without the evidence acquired through the hands, [the infant's] conception of objects – even when they are parts of his own body which themselves have sensory nerves that supply him with direct evidence – is incomplete.'

From the continuing efforts to touch, grasp and explore, we receive a constant flood of impressions and information which not only help us determine our place in the scheme of things, but reveal whether an object or person is a threat or is beneficial to our well-being and development.

Our sense of touch is essential to establishing primary relationships. As infants, our hands reach, grasp and hold onto our mother for sustenance, warmth and security. This primal experience of touching our mother (as well as our father) and being touched in return lays the foundation for nearly all of our attitudes towards other people – and our relationships with them – from that time onwards.

Because our hands can express so much of who we are, they play a primary role in our relationships as we grow older. A simple handshake can provide volumes of information about another person, and can tell us if he is warm, fearful, hostile, strong, friendly, supportive or weak, all within a fraction of a second. Because our hands express our 'heart energy' they can offer support, protection, comfort and affection. The sensation of being touched by someone who cares for us can be among the most satisfying experiences we can have. Without the hands, human relationship would be limited and one-dimensional.

The hands, of course, play a special role in sex. As children, our hands are used extensively to explore our bodies and help us discover the myriad of pleasant sensations (often to the embarrassment of our elders) the body holds for us. As we grow older, our hands provide us with our basic introduction to sexual pleasure, first with ourselves and then with others.

When we make love, the hands play a unique and important role. As our primary means of touch, the hands are used to explore the skin of the lover; to squeeze, rub, massage, press and scratch. We hold our lover's face in our hands, stroke their cheeks, and use the hands to lift, hug, grasp, hold and caress. By using our hands with creative exactitude, we can touch our partner in ways that can produce unparalleled sensations of ecstasy. After consummation, we continue to use our hands to caress, hug and squeeze our partner, prolonging the sense of pleasure and nurturing contact. Our hands provide the essential link of affection and intimacy so vital for an enduring romance.

Because of the special relationship between the human hand and sexual expression, psychological hand analysis can be a valuable tool to help us understand personal issues of sexuality, love and relationship. In addition to expressing ourselves on a concrete physical level through touch, our hands also reveal who we are symbolically by the shape, texture, mounts and lines.

In the context of sexual palmistry, the hands can reveal our basic level of vital force, and how it can translate into sexual energy, passion, commitment and our ability to love. They show our capacity for feeling, and can reveal mental and emotional blocks that can inhibit its flow. The hands help us determine our level of compatibility with others, and indicate how we can establish a relationship built on understanding and trust. Finally, by revealing traits, trends and abilities we may not be fully conscious of, the hands can help us transform whatever blocks us from achieving satisfying relationships, while

Figure 1.1: Heart and Hand Valentine, c.1850, artist unknown. From the collection of the American Museum of Folk Art, New York City.

enabling us to draw on many of our positive 'core' qualities which we may have overlooked.

Our book will be divided into three parts. The first section will provide a thorough grounding in the major theories behind psychosexual palmistry and its ability to provide important information regarding sex, love, and compatibility with others. Special attention will be given to hand shape, the fingers, and hand geography, which will include the mounts, lines, skin texture, hand motility and other characteristics.

The second part will deal with the basic components of sexuality and its expression. We will discuss the psychological aspects of sex and relationship, examine the varieties of sexual styles and how they can be seen in the hand, and explore the steps needed to achieve greater awareness and compatibility in our relationship with our partner.

The final section is devoted to the more practical aspects of hand reading. We will devote one chapter to the proper methods of reading hands, and will offer a variety of hand prints for analysis and discussion.

Chapter 2

THE FIVE TYPES
OF LOVER

The shape and overall appearance of the hand is a primary indicator of sexual personality, and over the years many palmists have attempted to classify the hands into distinct categories. While no one system is perfect – and few hands actually conform to one specific hand type – classifying the hands provides a general framework on which we can base a thorough hand analysis.

Basically, there are two general categories of hands which encompass all classifications: *receptive* and *realistic*. The receptive hand is often fragile and delicate in appearance, and is usually long and conic in shape, as seen in figure 2.1. Its owners tend to be highly sensitive, emotional and romantic. Generally speaking, their emotions are strongly evident in their relationships, which can manifest as powerful mood swings, dramatic outbursts, and emotional instability. A rich line pattern – signifying a highly complex personality and a tendency for nervousness – is common.

The realistic hand (figure 2.2) appears more outgoing and assertive. The hand is often strong and broad, giving an impression of substance and determination. Depending on the skin texture and consistency of the hand, the owner would be strongly

Figure 2.1: A 'receptive' hand

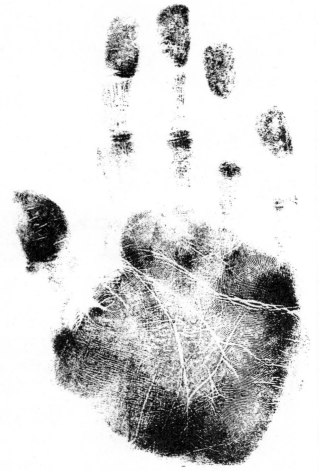

grounded in three-dimensional reality and would have strong interest in the physical aspects of sex.

As in *The Palmistry Workbook,* we will focus on four of the seven basic hand types first introduced by Captain Stanislaus d'Arpentigny in his book *La Science de la Main:* the square, spatulate, conic and psychic. We will also analyse the mixed hand classification, to which most people belong. In addition, we will discuss important modifying factors – including hand size, consistency, skin texture and flexibility – and see how they can provide important information about character and sexuality.

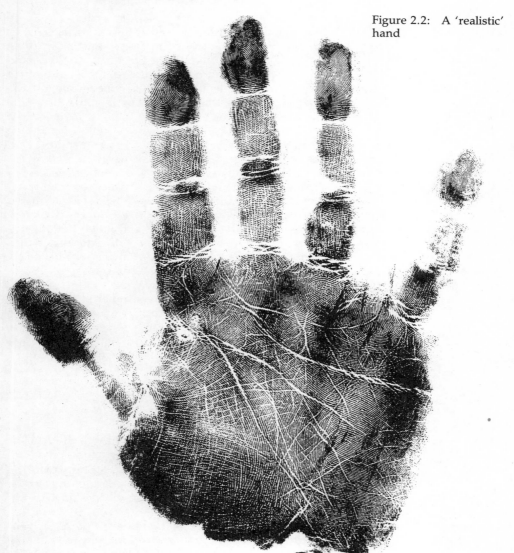

Figure 2.2: A 'realistic' hand

THE SQUARE HAND: ORDER!

The first category of the realistic classification is the square hand type (figure 2.3). Because it is squarish in form, it is called the hand of the organizer and planner.

21

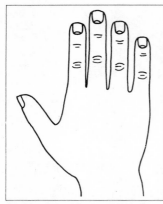

Figure 2.3: Square hand

People with squarish hands love order, constancy and stability. Common sense and reason tend to predominate over their emotions, and they often prefer a steady, systematic approach to love and relationship. When owners of squarish hands meet someone new, he or she may concentrate on the practical aspects of the potential relationship: 'Can she cook?' 'Will he be a good provider?', 'I wonder if she snores?', 'Will he develop a pot belly in ten years?' They will tend not to waste time with someone unless they are reasonably sure that the potential relationship has some chance of success, or fits into the image they have previously created about the kind of relationship they would like to have. However, once the choice is made to get involved, warmer, more loving feelings will move to the fore.

In a relationship, a person with squarish hands often has difficulty adapting to new circumstances, especially if the hand and/or thumb is rigid. Unless the head line droops towards the mount of Luna, they may also be rather conventional in their sexual habits, and can easily get caught up in routine. On the positive side, people with squarish hands are usually dependable, stable and patient with their partners, and are often able to cope well when confronted with difficult situations.

THE SPATULATE HAND: ACTION!

Spatulate hands (figure 2.4) also fall into the realistic category. They are often strong and broad in appearance, and are sometimes accompanied by slightly knotted fingers. Their outstanding visual quality is a marked 'fanning out' of the fingertips in the form of a spatula.

People with spatulate hands are energetic, self-confident and tenacious, and often know how to take advantage of an opportunity. While they possess the practical qualities of people with squarish hands, they love innovation, adventure and excitement in a relationship.

Owners of spatulate hands can be impulsive, charming, and exciting to be with. They can be infuriating as well, because they like to flirt, tease and act seductive with others even when they are in a

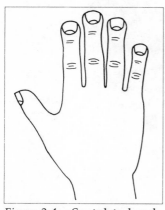

Figure 2.4: Spatulate hand

relationship. Unless other aspects of the hand modify the adventurous tendencies of a purely spatulate hand, there may be difficulties maintaining a committed relationship with one person, as such a hand indicates the potential of being involved with more than one person at a time.

People with spatulate hands are often highly sexed and can be sensual to the point of being hedonistic. When the hand is flexible and soft, the pursuit of physical pleasure can take precedence over other responsibilites like keeping an appointment, studying for exams, or even earning a living.

THE CONIC HAND: ROMANTIC!

Unlike the previous hand types, conic (or artistic) hands are of the receptive category. As seen in figure 2.5, they tend to be slightly tapered at the base of the palm and at the tips of the fingers. The skin texture is usually fine, revealing sensitivity and a love of beauty.

People with conic hands are frequently governed by impulse and first impressions. Unlike those with squarish hands, who are ruled by reason, owners of conic hands are more romantic, sentimental, impulsive and capricious in their relationships.

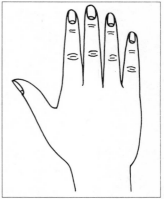

Figure 2.5: Conic hand

Inconsistency and instability are said to be major problems with those who possess conic hands. They can alternate between the proverbial 'peaks of exaltation and depths of despair', and can be intensely devoted to a partner one day and move on to someone else the next. However, if the hand is strong and firm, they will be more likely to commit themselves to a relationship and do what they can to make it endure.

Creativity is high. People with conic hands are often open, exciting and spontaneous in a relationship, and tend to dislike routine. Conic hands increase sexual versatility and innovation in the bedroom.

If the hand is firm and the lines well formed, creative energies tend to gravitate more towards intellectual pursuits. However, when the hand is bland and fat, the person's sensuous nature is especially strong. In addition to abundant food and drink, lots of sex and physical affection are counted among their primary needs in life.

THE PSYCHIC HAND: PAINFULLY IDEALISTIC

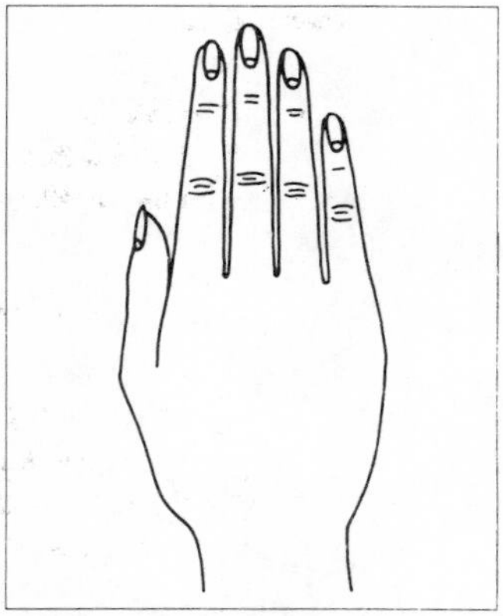

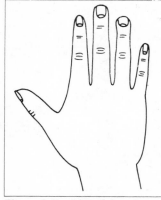

The psychic or intuitive hand (figure 2.6) is relatively rare, and features long graceful fingers and pointy tips. Like people with conic hands, owners of psychic hands are romantic, impressionable and emotional, but to a greater extent. People with psychic hands are often motivated by their deepest feelings, yet tend to lack reason and common sense. As a result, they are often highly idealistic and even naive in relationships, and can be out of touch with reality in the practical day-to-day work needed to make a relationship endure. For this reason, they need to attract strong, steady and sensitive partners who can help them 'ground' themselves in daily reality and to offer a greater sense of stability in their lives.

Figure 2.6: Psychic hand

THE MIXED HAND: ALL OF THE ABOVE

Very few hands actually conform to any of the previous hand types in their pure form, although one type may predominate over the others. For this reason we have a fifth classification – the mixed hand – which can provide an important frame of reference for an accurate psychosexual hand analysis.

By definition, the mixed hand (figure 2.7) contains aspects found in two or more of the previous hand types. The hand may be primarily square, yet one or two fingers may be spatulate in shape. The basic shape of the hand may be conic, yet it may also contain elements found in the more practical square hand.

The basic shape of the hand should serve as the foundation for a careful hand analysis. The fingers, mounts and lines, as well as modifiers like hand consistency and size, skin texture, and flexibility can often provide more specific information regarding psychosexual character analysis and individual sexual expression.

For these reasons we need to take *all* factors into account when we study a hand, and evaluate the

Figure 2.7: Mixed hand

relationships between the various aspects of the hand. While this may appear bewildering at first, you can accomplish this goal by cultivating intuition and patience. After some practice you can achieve a basic 'gestalt' of the hand after a few minutes of careful observation.

CONSISTENCY

Consistency of the hands is determined by measuring their hardness or softness under pressure. Understanding the basic consistency of the hand helps us determine the level of sexual energy and how it is expressed. By taking your friend's hands in yours and gently squeezing them, you can gain an accurate idea about their consistency.

The flesh of a *flabby hand* easily crushes when you squeeze gently. People with thin, flabby hands have low physical energy and are generally not very interested in having sex. They often have difficulty expressing their feelings and can give the impression of being emotionally 'flat'. In many cases, flabby hands are the indication of an idle, sensitive dreamer who dislikes both physical and emotional exertion.

When the hands are flabby and thick, the person will be more sensual. In addition to an increased appetite for sex, over-indulgence in food (and possibly drugs and alcohol) is indicated. If the thumb is small or bends back easily, will-power is often lacking.

Soft hands show a lack of bony feeling under pressure. While soft hands can also reveal a low sex drive, they offer more potential in this area than a flabby hand. However, when the hands are soft and thick (often giving the appearance of being pudgy) the sensuous nature is accentuated. Over-indulgence is common.

Elastic hands cannot be easily crushed by your grasp and tend to spring back under pressure. They reveal sexual vitality, adaptability and the capacity to respond (physically or otherwise) to new ideas and unusual situations.

Firm hands are slightly elastic and yield to moderate pressure. Generally speaking, they reveal a person who is physically active, psychologically stable and sexually potent. People with firm hands may have difficulty adapting to new and unexpected situations and tend to like events (and people) to conform to their own vision of things. However, with time, they can change their point of view.

Hard hands do not yield under pressure, and are often coarse in texture with no elasticity. Although people with hard hands (most of their owners are men) may have lots of physical strength and abundant sexual energy, they are often psychologically rigid and set in their ways. The openness and adaptability required for a successful relationship is often absent, and 'heart' feelings are often blocked. In addition, this withholding of energy can result in sudden outbursts of temper, especially if the hands and nails are reddish in colour.

FLEXIBILITY

Hand flexibility can be determined by the ease with which the hand can be bent backward. The degree of flexibility of the hand reveals one's ability to adapt to new circumstances and ideas.

A *very flexible hand* can bend back to a ninety-degree angle with a minimum of pressure. It reveals a person who is highly impressionable in a relationship and who can easily be controlled by others. At the same time, owners of very flexible hands often have difficulty being committed to one person and can be unpredictable in their attitudes and actions. If the thumb bends back easily as well, the person is generous to the extreme, and is often taken advantage of by people with more will-power and self-control.

A *moderately flexible hand* (figure 2.8) bends back in a graceful arc. People with this type of hand tend to be versatile on mental, emotional and sexual levels. Although they tend to be far more reliable than people with very flexible hands, they are able to adapt to new and unexpected situations. They are also fairly open with their feelings and have the ability to truly *give* to their partner in a relationship, especially if their hands are of a firm consistency. However, moderately flexible hands tend to indicate

Figure 2.8: Moderately flexible hand

more than one object of desire, so people with such hands may need to resolve issues of lack of commitment and faithfulness in their lives.

A *firm hand* hardly bends back at all under pressure. Although such a hand often reflects a healthy amount of vital force and strong sexual energy, its owners tend to be careful with their feelings and may withold emotionally from their partner until they feel safe and comfortable with them. They are rarely impulsive, and often need time to adapt to new ideas and unexpected situations.

A *stiff hand* (figure 2.9) is extremely rigid, and may actually turn inward in its natural state. Owners of stiff hands tend to be psychologically rigid, and are stubborn, inflexible and generally not very open to other opinions or new ideas. They want to have things *their way* in a relationship and find it difficult to compromise with their partner. While they may well experience deep affection and love, they often have difficulty sharing these 'heart' feelings with others. Anger is more easily expressed. On the more positive side, people with stiff hands are very reliable and responsible, and are excellent at keeping secrets.

Figure 2.9: Stiff hand

HAND SIZE

Although popular history has taught that the size of a person's open hand (measured from thumbtip to the tip of the little finger) corresponds with the size of their genitals, this has not been conclusively proven to be true. For our discussion on palmistry and sexuality, suffice to say that the relative size of the hand to the person's body size, weight and bone structure is more an indication of *character* rather than the size of their sexual equipment.

Generally speaking, *small hands* reveal an individual who views life on a grand scale. They are often intuitive and spontaneous, and harbour a basic aversion to details, unless their fingers are knotted. In relationships they tend to be more emotional than mental, and are guided more by their hunches than by reason. As lovers, they would tend to favour the dramatic, and would be primarily drawn to the purely erotic and physical aspects of sex.

On the opposite scale, people with *large hands*

appear to gravitate towards small things in life. They tend to be more analytical and mental in their relationships with others, and often rely on concrete details and facts when it comes to problem-solving. As lovers they would tend to be more attentive towards their partner, and would probably take a more relaxed, 'laid back' approach to love-making than people with small hands.

Unlike the apparently contradictory aspects of small and large hands, narrow and broad hands reveal corresponding aspects of the personality. When viewed in the context of love, sex and relationship, *narrow hands* reflect a narrow, restricted and often dogmatic view of life. Their owners tend to be rather conventional in sexual matters and are not very interested in new ideas and trends regarding sexuality and relationship. If a narrow hand is stiff and hard, the personality will probably be rigid and inflexible.

Figure 2.10: Fine skin texture

SKIN TEXTURE

The texture of the skin also corresponds with their emotional counterparts. The softer and finer the skin, the greater the physical and emotional sensitivity. People with fine skin (figure 2.10) are very sensitive to their surroundings and require an environment that is conducive to peace and harmony. In the context of a relationship, they are generally very aware of their affectional and emotional needs (and those of their partner). Ideally, they should seek a person whose hands also reveal signs of sensitivity. Consult chapter 7 for more discussion.

Coarse skin (figure 2.11) reflects a more 'rough and tumble' individual, who may not be strongly affected by the environment. Although modifying aspects may be present, people with coarse skin texture should strive to be more aware of their partner's needs and try to develop a more receptive nature.

During the past few years, an increasing number of palmists have discovered that skin ridge patterns or *dermoglyphics* on the palm and fingertips can be reliable indicators of certain physical and emotional conditions. In figure 2.11, the vast majority of the

Figure 2.11: Coarse skin texture

skin ridges are clear and well-formed. However, when the majority of skin ridges are ill-formed and disassociated (figure 2.12) a 'string of pearls' is present, and can lead to a predisposition towards neurosis.

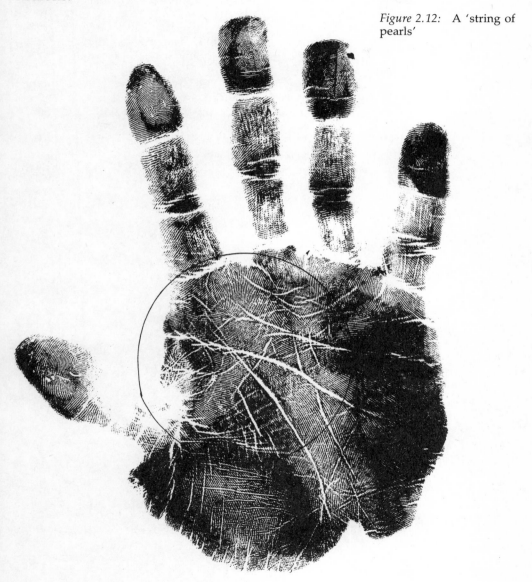

Figure 2.12: A 'string of pearls'

RIGHT OR LEFT?

When we examine a person's hands, we need to discover which of the two is dominant. The non-dominant or *passive* hand reflects our past and innate potential, while the dominant or *active* hand shows primarily what we are doing with our lives at the moment. Very often, the hands reveal marked differences between our innate potential and the degree to which it is being fulfilled.

Generally speaking, the dominant hand is the one with which we write. In the rare instances where a person is ambidextrous and writes with both hands, we need to observe both hands together. When the hands are different, we should ask questions as we proceed with the reading in order to discover which of the two hands is the more reliable indicator of the person's life.

Chapter 3

THE FINGERS

The fingers of the hand offer a wealth of specific information concerning both our sexual personality and major avenues of sexual expression. In fact, some chirologists feel that the fingers can tell us more about the sexuality of a person than any other single aspect of the hand.

When studying the fingers, it is important to study each finger by itself and also as an integral part of the hand. In addition, we must also understand the relationship of each finger to the others. We can determine a finger's relative strength in the hand by opening the hand completely, with fingers held together. If the fingers lean towards one in particular, that finger is the dominant finger in the hand and provides us with the key-note of the individual's character.

Before we discuss the characteristics of each individual finger, it is important to become familiar with the appearances of the fingers in general.

Flexibility: Like the hands, the degree of flexibility of the fingers provides important clues to the person's character and its ability to adapt. Ideally, fingers should arch gently backward, revealing a capacity to adapt easily to new ideas and situations. Stiff fingers betray a more rigid personality, which

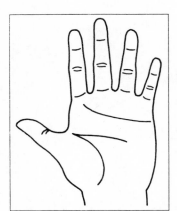

Figure 3.1: Hand with short fingers

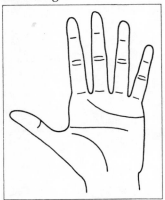

Figure 3.2: Hand with long fingers

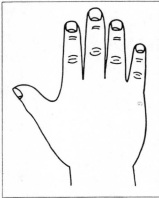

Figure 3.3: Hand with smooth fingers

would tend to be socially and sexually conservative. When the top phalange of the finger bends back, strong creative talent is often present. When the tip of the Mercury finger bends back, for example, strong communication skills are evident.

Length and width: The length of the fingers should be considered in relation to the length of the palm. A balance exists if the size of the middle of the Saturn finger were the same length as the palm itself.

Generally speaking, people with short fingers (figure 3.1) rely more on their instincts than on analysis and detail. They are intuitive, impulsive and impatient. In a relationship, people with short fingers are able to quickly understand the essence of an issue or problem, and are able to perceive any hidden meanings within a conversation. Unless their fingers are knotted, they tend to dislike details and view life on a large, overall scale.

Long fingers (figure 3.2) indicate opposite qualities. Patience, love of detail and the tendency to analyse are among their common psychological traits. Unlike their short-fingered counterparts, they are more introspective than not, and can harbour grudges and resentment when they feel slighted, hurt or betrayed.

The thicker and fleshier the fingers, the greater the sensuality. People with thick fingers enjoy rich food, luxurious surroundings, and, of course, lots of sex. Thin, bony fingers tend to reveal a more intellectual and less sensate person, who is often removed from the world of sensuous pleasure.

Knuckles: Smooth fingers (figure 3.3) have an absence of developed joints, and indicate a tendency to be intuitive and impulsive. People with smooth fingers often have difficulty breaking down a problem into its component parts and are impatient with details. Their decisions are based primarily on hunches rather than a careful examination of the facts. In a relationship, they are often in touch with their feelings and find it easy to express their anger, love or joy.

If the fingers are both short and smooth, impulsiveness, impatience and aversion to detail are accentuated, while long fingers will tend to strengthen the intellectual and analytical aspects of the personality. Decision-making can be slow.

Knotty fingers which are not due to arthritis (figure 3.4) reveal a person with a strong analytical mind. Their owners are rarely seduced by appearances, and tend to be cautious when it comes to developing new relationships with others. People with knotty fingers may also lack spontaneity and find it difficult to express their feelings to others.

The phalanges: The index, middle, ring and little fingers are divided into three parts or *phalanges* (figure 3.5). The top phalange is that of mental order, the middle phalange is that of practical order, while the bottom phalange is called the phalange of material order.

When the top phalange is the longest of the three, it is an indication that mental activities absorb much of the person's attention. A long middle phalange indicates that the primary keynote – as expressed by the particular finger's significance – is action. A long and often thick phalange of material order reflects that the person is more grounded in the sensate or material aspects of life. Remember that the comparative length and thickness of the phalanges will probably vary from finger to finger.

Before we proceed to the individual fingers, let us recapitulate the key qualities of the various types:

Spatulate (figure 3.6): adventurous, physically active, impulsive, down to earth, sensual.

Square (figure 3.7): loves order, systematic, stable, conventional, dependable, rational.

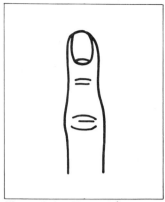
Figure 3.4: Knotty finger

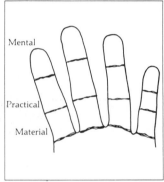
Figure 3.5: The three phalanges of the fingers – Mental, Practical, Material

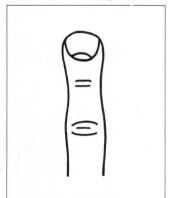
Figure 3.6: Spatulate finger

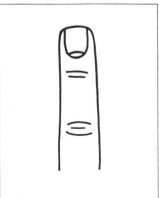
Figure 3.7: Square finger

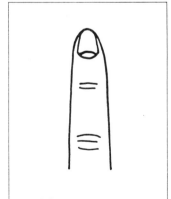
Figure 3.8: Conic finger

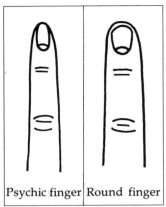

| Psychic finger | Round finger |

Figure 3.9:   *Figure 3.10:*

Conic (figure 3.8): creative, romantic, receptive to outer stimuli, inconsistent, versatile, instinctive.

Psychic (figure 3.9): strongly affected by outside stimuli, very idealistic, highly sensitive, impractical, emotional.

Round (figure 3.10): Adaptable, well-rounded, active yet receptive, mental yet emotional, balanced.

Many hands are a combination of these types, so we need to take into account both the qualities governing each finger as well as the finger's basic form. Now let us consider each finger individually.

THE THUMB

In the context of sexuality and relationship, the thumb relates to our ego strength and our level of sexual energy and sexual capacity. Because the thumb enables us to accomplish a wide variety of practical tasks in daily life, it also symbolizes our ability to express this energy and power in the world.

The size of the thumb is an index to the basic energy level of the individual. Normally, the tip of the thumb should reach to the lower phalange of the index or Jupiter finger. A long thumb (figure 3.11) indicates an abundance of sexual energy in addition to a forceful personality. Their owners are often egocentric and domineering in relationships, and like to be the centre of attention. People with short

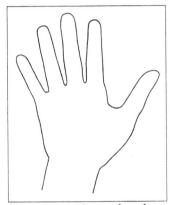

Figure 3.11:   Long thumb

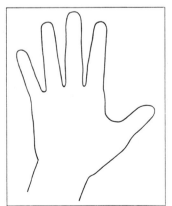

Figure 3.12:   Short thumb

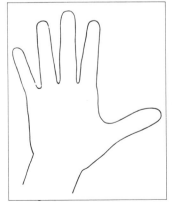

Figure 3.13:   Low-set thumb

thumbs (figure 3.12) tend to be weak-willed and are not known for their strong or imposing character.. They often lack self-confidence and forcefulness, and can be dominated by their partner in a relationship.

However, before we proclaim a thumb to be long or short, we need to take account of how the thumb is set on the hand. A *low-set thumb* can be positioned at a ninety-degree angle, as shown in figure 3.13. It reveals a person who is self-confident, independent, and who takes risks in life. People with low-set thumbs tend to be unconventional and spontaneous in their approach to sex and relationship. To the degree that the thumb is placed high on the hand (figure 3.14) the person tends to be more repressed and withholding on emotional and sexual levels. They would tend to be Victorian in sexual tastes, and will be afraid to 'let go' and flow with the rhythm of life. However, it is important to remember that a high-set thumb can be modified by other aspects of the hand, such as a separation between the lines of life and head at their commencement, or a hand and thumb which are more flexible than firm. When the thumb is set at a sixty-degree angle, there is more of a balance between these two extremes. There may still be a degree of sexual repression and fear of experimentation, but it is not as acute as the owner of the high-set thumb.

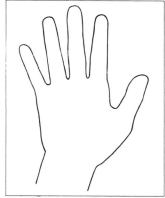

Figure 3.14: Thumb set high

The thumb itself is divided into three parts, as shown in figure 3.15. The nail phalange is called the *phalange of will* while the second is the *phalange of logic*. The third part is the *mount of Venus*, which is a primary indicator of our capacity for love and sexual expression. It will be discussed in the following chapter.

A strong phalange of will – one that is well-rounded, long and wide – indicates decisiveness, tenacity and the ability to translate thought into action. When this phalange is conic in shape, the person's energy can scatter and the individual would have difficulty dealing effectively with a problem requiring persistence and long-term attention. If this phalange is thin or flat (when viewed from the side) the person will be highly strung and nervous. When the thumbtip is squarish, the person's approach to relationship will be practical and rational, while a spatulate thumbtip would reveal an instinctual

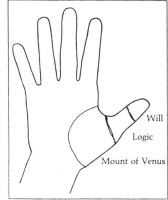

Figure 3.15: The three phalanges of the thumb

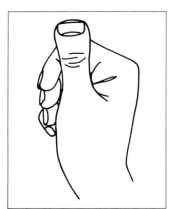

Figure 3.16: 'Murderer's thumb

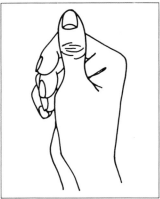

Figure 3.17: Waisted thumb

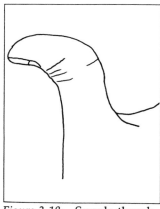

Figure 3.18: Supple thumb

approach to relationship based more on sexual or affectional feelings than rational thought and analysis. In general, people with spatulate thumbs are very dynamic and exciting to be with. Things 'happen' around them.

A very small number of people have a thumb with a deformed will phalange which has a bulbous or clubbed appearance (figure 3.16). Traditionally, palmists have called it a 'murderer's thumb' and while it does not normally indicate homicidal tendencies, it is often a sign that the person tends to withhold energy to such an extent that strong, sudden bursts of temper can result. People with such thumbs must be treated with tact and sensitivity. When a clubbed thumb is found on a coarse hand with reddish skin, the person can become violent and has the potential for being a spouse or child abuser. Check the entire hand for modifying influences before arriving at conclusions, however.

The phalange of logic reveals our degree of reasoning power in a relationship. Ideally, it should be of the same length and strength as the phalange of will, indicating a balance between thought and action. To the extent that this phalange is long and thick, the ego will exert strong control over action to the point that excessive reason can hinder movement altogether. This is especially true if the thumb joint is knotted. When the logic phalange is 'waisted' (figure 3.17) the person is more likely to follow instinct than logic in making decisions. In addition, some palmists believe that a 'waisted thumb' is a sign of tact in social and business situations.

The flexibility of the thumb is also important. A supple thumb (figure 3.18) bends back at the joint, and reveals emotional versatility and a capacity to adapt well to other people and in social situations. People with flexible thumbs can also be very generous with their loved ones, whether in affection or material objects. When the thumb is extremely flexible (i.e. bending back ninety degrees or more) the person can be generous to a fault, and can easily be used by others. He can also be extravagant with money, especially if the rest of the hand is very flexible as well. Will-power can be minimal, and the person may have difficulty being faithful in a relationship.

A moderately flexible thumb bends back only slightly under pressure. In relationships, people with this type of thumb rely more on common sense than on instinct. While they may be open-minded and willing to adapt to being with another person, they can also be strong-willed and tenacious when they need to be.

Stiff thumbs (figure 3.19) will not bend back under pressure. Their owners tend to be stubborn, prudent, and have difficulty accommodating other people's likes and dislikes in the context of a relationship. Unless the rest of the hand bends back somewhat, they can be rigid, inflexible and withholding of feelings. On the more positive side, people with stiff thumbs are generally stable and responsible and can be relied upon for almost anything.

Each of the other fingers has a name, and characterizes the type of energy that is channelled through it. Each finger is named after a heavenly body, which is, in turn, named after Greek or Roman gods and goddesses. They represent aspects of our character that are symbolized by these mythological beings.

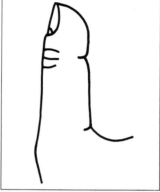

Figure 3.19: Stiff thumb

JUPITER

The index or Jupiter finger is named after Jupiter or Zeus, the King of the gods. The essential qualities of this finger reflect the outgoing qualities of life: ambition, charisma, inspiration, leadership, magnanimity. Ideally, this finger should reach the middle of the top phalange of the Saturn finger and be equal in length to the Apollo finger.

If Jupiter is longer than Apollo and reaches past the midpoint of the top phalange of Saturn, the person is a natural leader and likes to take charge in relationships. At the same time, a long and strong Jupiter finger can accent the tendency to be vain, domineering and controlling. If other factors of the hand are present, there may be a psychological need for sexual conquests. In general, there is a big ego, with a deep inner level of self-esteem. To the extent that Jupiter is shorter than Apollo, there is a corresponding lack of self-esteem and self-confidence, especially if the head and life lines are joined.

When Jupiter bends towards Saturn, the positive core qualities of the finger are distorted, and the tendency to be possessive and jealous is indicated. When the fingertip is pointed, the person tends to be idealistic in love; when the finger is squarish, a more pragmatic approach to love is often indicated.

SATURN

The middle finger is named for the god Saturn, the Judge, and is the finger of propriety, responsibility and introspection. Saturn in the hand serves as the link between the subconscious aspects of the personality represented by Apollo and Mercury and the more actively conscious qualities represented by the thumb and Jupiter finger.

When the Saturn finger is straight, there is harmony between will and emotion, as well as a balance between liking to be with people and wanting to be alone. When Saturn curves slightly towards Jupiter, the person is basically spontaneous and outgoing, and enjoys being in the company of others most of the time. A slight curve towards Apollo indicates a tendency towards melancholy and a preference for being alone more than not. This should not be interpreted as being anti-social, however. Although people with such fingers need 'their own space', they also enjoy social situations and partnerships. A sharp curve towards Apollo is a certain indicator of chronic depression. This will be discussed further in chapter 7.

APOLLO

The ring or Apollo finger is named for the god of power and self-expression. It rules creativity, a love of art and music, and the ability to express our thoughts and feelings to others. As we mentioned earlier, the length of Apollo and Jupiter should be roughly equal, and like Jupiter, the Apollo finger should ideally extend as far as the middle of the top phalange of Saturn. This would highlight the finest qualities of Apollo, and would indicate self-esteem, self-confidence, and a feeling of well-being in the world. However, if the Apollo finger is longer, there may be a corresponding lack of self-esteem. In some cases, the owner may not stand up for himself in a relationship and can be dominated by his partner. However, this tendency can be modified by a firm mount of Upper Mars, or lines of head and life that do not join at their commencement.

Generally speaking, people with a well-formed and strong Apollo finger make bright and interesting companions. They have a flair for nice clothes and tend to fit in well in social situations. When Apollo is straight, the individual is a good judge of others, and his relationships tend to be grounded in reality. However, when Apollo bends towards Saturn, the person may tend to overestimate others and become disillusioned when they don't live up to his high standards. According to some chirologists, an Apollo finger which bends sharply towards Saturn (not due to arthritis or injury) is a sign of a gambler and libertine.

A spatulate tip on the Apollo finger increases one's communication skills and the ability to relate well to others, especially in groups. This is especially true when the Mercury finger is long.

MERCURY

Mercury was the messenger of the gods. For this reason, the little or Mercury finger rules the ability to communicate with others, both in public as well as in intimate relationships. Ideally, this finger should reach the top phalange of the Apollo finger. The longer the finger, the greater the ability to relate to others. When this finger is short, very often it is difficult making oneself understood. In many cases, this makes it very difficult to establish and maintain long-term relationships.

A straight Mercury finger indicates honesty, trustworthiness, and perhaps a tendency to be naive both in business and in romance. A slight curve towards Apollo will add a degree of astuteness and diplomacy, while a sharp bending towards Apollo (again, not caused by arthritis or injury) indicates a tendency to be manipulative and even dishonest in relationships. When this bending is accompanied by a sharply bending Jupiter finger towards Saturn, there is the potential that the individual would stop at nothing to obtain what he or she wants.

FINGER SPACING

When the fingers of the hand are held closely together when the hand is open, the individual tends to be somewhat fearful of life and to lack self-confidence and independence in relationships. The wider the spacing between the fingers, the greater the openness, daring and independence.

When the Jupiter finger breaks away from the hand, leadership and self-reliance are increased. The person tends to take charge and want to make all the decisions in a relationship. The Australian palmist Andrew Fitzherbert notes that when a short Jupiter finger breaks away from Saturn, the person would tend to hide feelings of inadequacy and insecurity by drawing attention to himself in social situations.

A wide spacing between the Saturn and Apollo fingers can indicate unconventionality. In some cases, it may also reveal a split personality which makes it difficult for others to understand the individual's real nature.

To the degree that the space between Apollo and Mercury is wide, the person is unconventional in their views about sexuality and relationship. Look to other aspects of the hand for confirming or modifying traits.

NAILS

The nails are also helpful in determining character and how we relate to others. Long, broad and slightly rounded nails are a sign of openness, broad-mindedness and a non-critical nature. Long, narrow nails – when not modified by other indicators on the hand – point towards suspicion, selfishness, and a tendency to be narrow-minded and calculating in relationships. Short nails (not caused by nail-biting) reveal a critical individual who not only focuses on the perceived shortcomings of others, but is often very critical of himself as well. He often sabotages or downplays his own talents and positive character traits, when they in fact deserve recognition and expression.

Nail colour is primarily an indicator of sexual vitality. People with reddish nails tend to have a strong sex drive and are more able to express this passion in purely physical terms. However, they are also prone to flashes of intense anger and need to create outlets (other than sex) for the excess energy.

Bright pink nails tend to modify this strong sex drive, and their owners tend to enjoy more of a balance between the physical and emotional expressions of love and passion. Their nails reveal good circulation, body warmth and an outgoing, affectionate character.

People with bluish nails (especially if there are no complaints about poor circulation) are somewhat cold and reserved, and have difficulty expressing their affection in a physical way. Although they do not lack passion and strong love feelings, they often need some time to 'warm up' to someone in a relationship. Pale nails – like pale skin – indicate low physical vitality and minimal sex drive, unless modified by other hand characteristics.

Chapter 4

HAND TOPOGRAPHY I: THE MOUNTS

The regions and mounts of the hand can be compared to the mountains, valleys and plains of the Earth. Like hand shape, flexibility and the fingers, the regions and mounts have much to say about personality traits, innate sexual energy and our primary modes of sexual expression.

The hand is divided into six primary zones and then into eight mounts, very much like the division of a geographic region into counties and towns. While the six zones provide a general orientation regarding latent capacities and outward expression, the eight mounts reveal the far more specialized information we need for a thorough psychosexual character analysis.

THE LONGITUDINAL ZONES

The three longitudinal zones are formed by drawing an imaginary vertical line from a point between the index and middle fingers downwards towards the wrist, and another to the wrist from a point between the middle and ring fingers, as shown in figure 4.1.

The first division forms the *active conscious* zone, which represents the energy we consciously apply in our dealings with the material world. It relates to the assertion of the ego in daily life on both intellectual and concrete levels. It is the region of practical knowledge, outward movement, and the application of principles in our work, study and relationships.

The zone located on the opposite third of the hand represents our hidden energy reserve, or the *passive subconscious*. It relates more to our innate creativity, emotional awareness and instinctual capacity.

The middle zone, or *zone of balance*, serves as a meeting place where these different energies can blend. This is an area where we often find the line of Saturn or line of life task, which moves up from the base of the palm towards the middle finger. It speaks of career, movement in life, and the degree to which we have found our task or niche in the world.

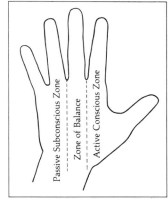

Figure 4.1: The longitudinal zones of the hand.

THE LATITUDINAL ZONES

The three latitudinal zones (figure 4.2) are formed by drawing a horizontal line from the tip of the thumb across to a point below the base of the fingers, and another from just above the thumb ball directly across the palm.

The first division, or the *emotional/conscious* zone, represents our active link with the world around us. Depending on the mounts which lie within this area, it is the zone of emotional expression, the application of power, inspiration, ambition, artistic creation and business acumen. According to Walter Sorell, it is the area of the hand that has the keenest sense of touch and holds the strongest power of connection with objects and people.

The lower region or *instinctive subconscious* zone, is the zone of the Freudian 'id' and our primary motivating forces. Depending on the mounts which lie within it, this zone relates to intuition, imagination, libido and our deepest, most hidden desires.

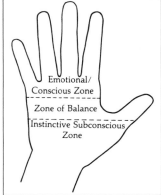

Figure 4.2: The latitudinal zones of the hand.

Like the vertical middle zone mentioned earlier, the middle horizontal zone is the practical zone of *balance*. It is the region of logic, common sense and reason, and represents the blending of thought and feeling. It is the area which filters and absorbs our subconscious drives and helps guide them towards concrete expression. It integrates our aspirations and intellectual abilities with our physical and instinctual drives.

THE MOUNTS

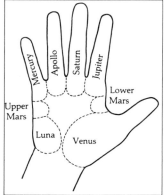

Figure 4.3: The mounts of the hand

Figure 4.4: The apex of the mount

Each of the mounts (figure 4.3) has a name, and characterizes the type of energy that is channelled through that part of the hand. Like most of the fingers, the mounts are named after planets, which are, in turn, named after Greek or Roman gods and goddesses. They represent aspects of our character that are symbolized by these mythological beings.

The strength of a particular mount depends on its relative size when compared with the other mounts of the hand. The more directly the mount is centred under the corresponding finger, the greater its strength and influence on our sexual personality. You can determine the displacement of the mount by locating its *apex*. The apex of a mount is found where the ridges of the skin meet to form a pattern, as seen in figure 4.4. If the apex of the Saturn mount, for example, is located more towards the mount of Apollo, it will take on some of the characteristics of the Apollo mount.

It should be remembered that the strength of a particular mount can be modified by other aspects of the hand, such as the shape and strength of the corresponding finger as well as the clarity and strength of both major and minor lines.

JUPITER

When the size of this mount is in harmonious balance with the other mounts, it reveals a good level of self-esteem and the positive aspects of Jupiter in relationship: healthy self-assertion, idealism, devotion, and the desire to move out to others and get involved with them. If this mount is unusually strong and prominent, ambition, egotism, vanity and pride are strong aspects of the personality. In relationships, the person tends to be overbearing and domineering and to insist on making all the decisions involving both partners. If this mount is deficient or flat, the person is likely to have a poor self-image and may also lack the positive self-assertion so necessary in a balanced relationship. Unless modified by other aspects in the hand, the person tends to feel awkward in social situations and has difficulty establishing new relationships with others.

SATURN

A normal sized mount of Saturn reveals a lover of independence and responsibility, who is able to balance the desire to be alone with the need to share the company of others. Fidelity, constancy, introspection, prudence and analysis are some of the keywords which describe the qualities of a normal Saturn mount.

A highly developed or large mount can distort these basic qualities, especially if strengthened by other hand characteristics. Prudence can yield to fearful withdrawal, and healthy introspection can be overshadowed by a tendency to be overly analytical and self-absorbed. A strong Saturn mount – unless it is modified by other factors like a flexible hand or thumb – can be found on people who are rigid, taciturn and defensive in their dealings with others.

APOLLO

Like its corresponding finger, the mount of Apollo rules creativity and self-expression. A medium-sized mount reveals a love of beauty and the ability to create. This creativity need not be limited to painting a picture or playing a musical instrument, but can be expressed in cooking, running a household, or making love. Generally speaking, people with a good Apollo mount know how to dress well, are born entertainers, and have a sense of style in their lives. They make charming and interesting companions, as well as good sexual partners. Check the mount of Venus for collaborating or modifying factors.

Like the mounts of Jupiter and Saturn, a very large mount of Apollo can both strengthen and distort its basic 'core' qualities. A preoccupation with pleasure, wealth or fame is often revealed by a very prominent

Apollo mount. A strong love of beauty can become a devotion to appearance values and living on the periphery. Vanity and self-indulgence can replace the natural desire to look after our appearance and take good care of ourselves.

When this mount is weak, the individual may be lacking the essential Apollonian qualities. Instead of being exciting and filled with beauty, the person's life can be ascetic, boring and 'flat'. A deficiency in this mount can also indicate low physical energy, and hence, a reduced sex drive.

MERCURY

Figure 4.5: Samaritan lines on the mount of Mercury

Mercury was the messenger of the gods, and the mount of Mercury, located under the little finger, rules communication. A well-developed mount favours oratorical skill and the ability to relate well to both individuals and groups. Like a long, well-developed Mercury finger, a good mount increases our capacity to relate well to our partner on verbal, emotional and sexual levels. A small, flat Mercury mount (especially when accompanied by a short finger) may hinder our ability to communicate with others on a one-to-one basis, especially in the context of an affective relationship.

A series of small vertical lines on the mount of Mercury are known as *samaritan lines* (figure 4.5). Often found on the hands of doctors, therapists and other members of 'helping professions', they indicate a natural healing ability on both physical and emotional levels. People whose hands feature samaritan lines tend to be nurturing and caring in their relationships, and often attract people who instinctively need their help.

MARS

There are two mounts of Mars on the hand, and both represent the dynamic, egotistical and separative aspects of the human personality. These mounts speak of our desire to survive, to succeed in life, and to overcome obstacles and difficulties.

The *upper mount of Mars* is located just under the

mount of Mercury, and symbolizes determination and resistance. When it is well-formed and firm to the touch, it betrays courage and bravery. Their owners hate to be manipulated or otherwise 'pushed around' by others. People with small or soft mounts often have difficulty standing up for their rights in a relationship. They tend to be dominated by their partners, especially if their hands and thumbs are flexible and of soft or bland consistency.

Unlike the upper mount of Mars which symbolizes passive resistance, the *lower mount of Mars* reveals the more active and outgoing Martial qualities of courage and self-assertion. Located between the mounts of Jupiter and Venus (see below), it sometimes appears as a small pad or tumour just inside the thumb joint. A well-formed mount reflects the ability to face the challenges of life and to take the initiative with other people in social situations.

When this mount is large and hard, the person has a strong temper in addition to strong sexual passions. When this mount is reddish and appears on a hand with coarse skin texture, it indicates a tendency towards violence, which can be directed towards spouse and children. A small or deficient mount (it can hardly be seen) indicates a basically quiet, passive and self-effacing individual who rarely can become angry with others.

VENUS

Named after the goddess of love, the mount of Venus is the primary indicator of love, passion and sex drive in the hand. It speaks of vitality, the capacity for friendship and the ability to love.

Ideally, this mount comprises the entire thumb ball and is outlined by a widely sweeping life line. It should take up approximately one-third of the palmar surface, and be neither too hard nor too bland. Smooth and firm to the touch, it should be higher than the other mounts in elevation, and slightly pink in colour. Such a mount reflects vitality, warmth and passion, as well as a strong capacity to love and receive love from others.

When this mount is excessively large in relation to the other mounts (figure 4.6) there is an abundance of

Figure 4.6: A very large and prominent mount of Venus

physical passion, with a large appetite for sex. When this mount is also reddish and hard to the touch, this passion can easily spill over into aggression and brutality, especially if the skin texture is coarse.

A small, flat or weak Venus mount reveals a lack of vital force and physical passion. The personality tends to be somewhat lymphatic and cold, especially if the mount is intersected by the life line (which begins at the edge of the palm, between thumb and Jupiter finger, and arcs down towards the wrist). Very often the size of this mount can change. A strong love affair has been known to increase the size of the mount of Venus, while prolonged periods of loneliness can decrease it.

LUNA

Located opposite the mount of Venus just above the wrist, the mount of Luna represents the passive, receptive and emotional aspects of the personality. It is the home of our subconscious impressions and unconscious drives, instinct and imagination.

Ideally, this mount should be broad and slightly rounded in shape. People with a rounded and moderately sized lunar mount let their instincts guide them in relationships more than mental reasoning, especially if small lines of intuition move up this mount diagonally towards the centre of the hand.

The stronger and more prominent the mount, the greater the imagination and subconscious drives, particularly if the head line slopes downward towards Luna. A large and prominent mount can also reflect a strong desire to nurture and protect others, especially when accompanied by the samaritan lines (figure 4.5) mentioned earlier.

However, if a large lunar mount is accompanied by a long and strong Jupiter finger, the individual's protective instincts can express themselves by wanting to dominate over others 'for their own good'. When the mount is deficient or lacking, the person tends to be realistic to the point of being unimaginative or even dull. If the mount of Venus is small as well, the person may tend to be detached and aloof in relationships. However, be sure to examine the entire hand for confirming or modifying factors.

Chapter 5

HAND TOPOGRAPHY II: THE LINES

The lines on the hand can be compared to the motorways, highways and country lanes of a road map. They indicate the major talents and energies we have at our disposal, our capacity to manifest these talents in life, and the probable directions in which these talents and energies will take us. In essence, the lines of the hand form a natural map of our life course, while allowing for occasional detours and changes of direction according to our free will.

The lines in the hand can change in a matter of weeks, although most changes can be observed every year or so. They are affected by both attitude modification and changes in behaviour. Learning how to meditate, cutting down on cigarettes, or devoting more time and energy to making a relationship work can alter the lines of the hand dramatically. For those interested in achieving their full potential – whether in career, health or relationships – the objective knowledge offered by the ever-changing lines can be both valuable and exciting. The lines show that we are indeed the 'master of our fate' and can assume personal responsibility for our life and its direction.

LINE QUALITY AND QUANTITY

Ideally, lines should be clear and well-defined, and have a colour complementing that of the skin. The lines' depth and width should be even. A particularly deep line reveals excessive energy, while a broad, shallow line indicates a lack of strength and focus. Generally speaking, the stronger the line, the stronger its influence.

The number of lines on the hand is also important.

Figure 5.1: The major lines of the hand

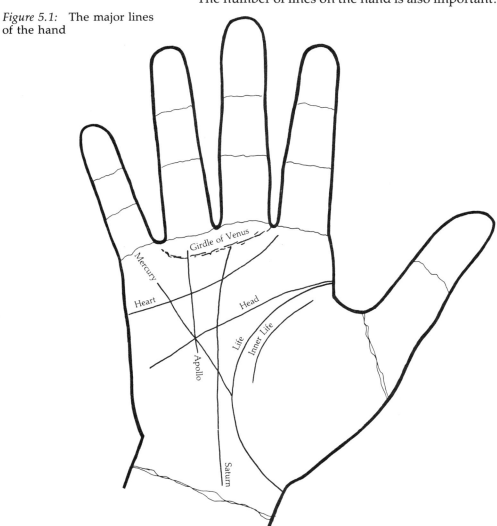

An abundance of lines indicates hypersensitivity and nervousness. It can also show that the individual has many paths in life through which to express his or her talents. Having few lines on the hand generally indicates little sensitivity, with few basic channels for life expression.

There are four major lines and nine minor lines on the hand, as seen in figures 5.1 and 5.2. They are discussed in detail in *The Palmistry Workbook,* so we will not repeat the same information here. However, in the context of our study on palmistry, sex and

Figure 5.2: The minor lines

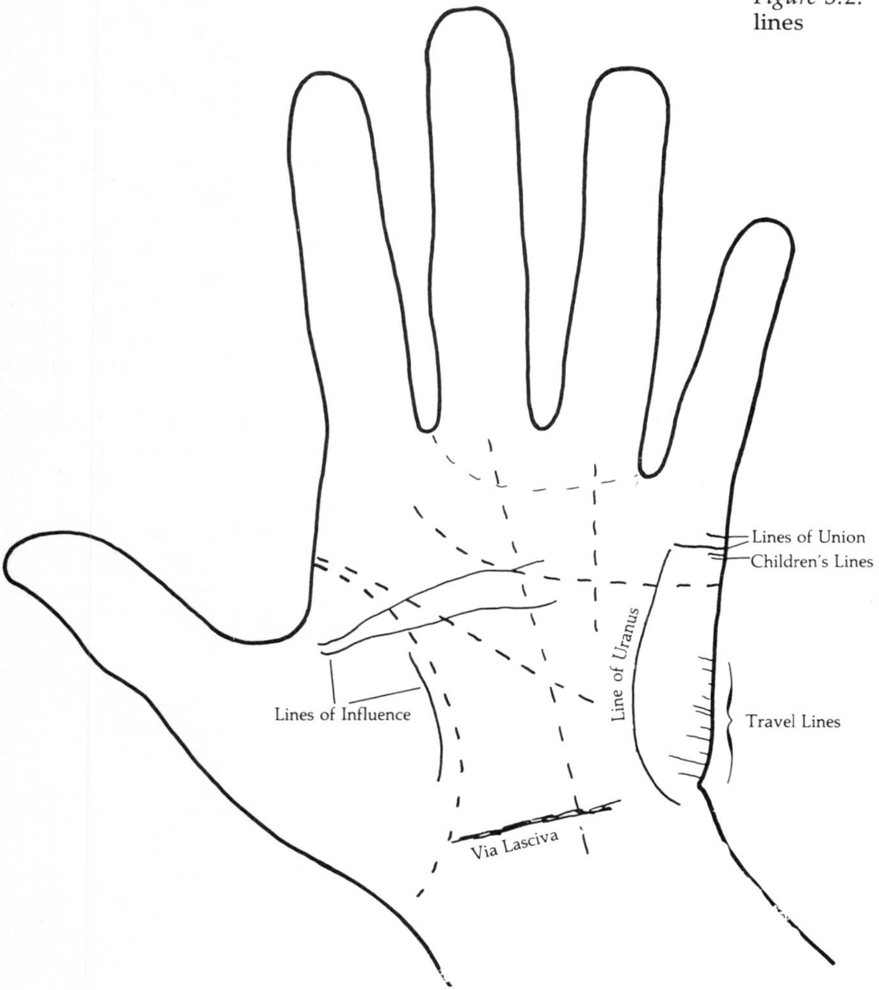

Lines of Union
Children's Lines

Line of Uranus

Lines of Influence

Travel Lines

Via Lasciva

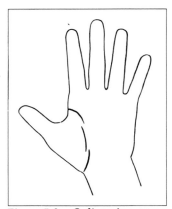

Figure 5.3: Splintering or splitting of a line

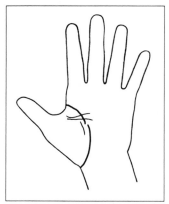

Figure 5.4: Lines of influence

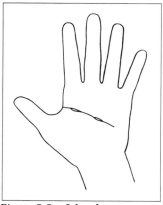

Figure 5.5: Islands

relationship, some lines merit a more specialized analysis because they offer unique information regarding our sexual personality and factors which help determine its expression.

Before we go into detail about each of the lines, there are several important formations we need to be familiar with.

Splintering or *splitting* of a line (figure 5.3) dissipates its strength and focus. In some cases, a split indicates a new phase in a person's life, so its existence is not necessarily a negative sign.

Lines of influence (figure 5.4) are small lines which cross or run parallel to the major lines. Lines which run parallel to vertical lines strengthen those lines. In many cases, they repair a split or strengthen a section of a line that is islanded or chained. Lines of influence also emanate from the mount of Venus. Generally speaking, they indicate obstacles, traumas and times of testing. They are not necessarily negative in meaning, and often record events which provide wisdom and life experience. If, at the point of crossing a line (usually the life and/or head lines) a red dot is formed, a major illness or accident is possible. This would also hold true if an island or break follows the point of crossing. Examine other lines for confirming or modifying indicators.

Islands (figure 5.5) form where there is a splitting from a line which reunites with that line later on. Islands impair the line's strength and indicate a lack of focus or dissipation of energy.

A *chain* (figure 5.6) is composed of many islands together, and indicates a prolonged period of vacillation and scattered energy. The line as a whole is weakened as a result.

A *fork* (figure 5.7) appears at the end of a line when the line splits. Depending on its location, it can either indicate a dissipation of the basic energies represented in the line, or can reveal balance and adaptability.

A *dot* (figure 5.8) appears as a slight coloured indentation on the line. The existence of a dot indicates a physical or emotional setback of some kind, depending on its colour and location.

A *grille* (figure 5.9) is formed by numerous fine lines which criss-cross each other. It generally indicates diffused or scattered energy. In the context of our discussion, its presence on the mount of Venus reveals a tendency for sexual excess, especially if the mount is reddish in colour.

A *square* (figure 5.10) is formed by four independent lines which create a rectangle. It is a sign of protection and preservation and often repairs a broken line.

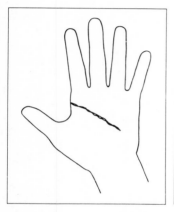

Figure 5.6: A chained line

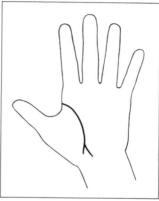

Figure 5.7: A forked line

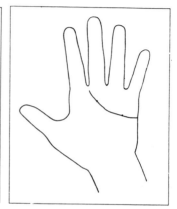

Figure 5.8: A 'dotted' line

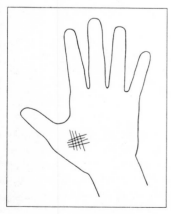

Figure 5.9: Lines forming a 'grille'

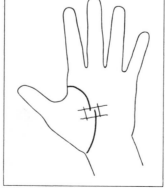

Figure 5.10: Lines forming a 'square'

THE LINE OF LIFE

Figure 5.11: Gauging time on the major lines of the hand

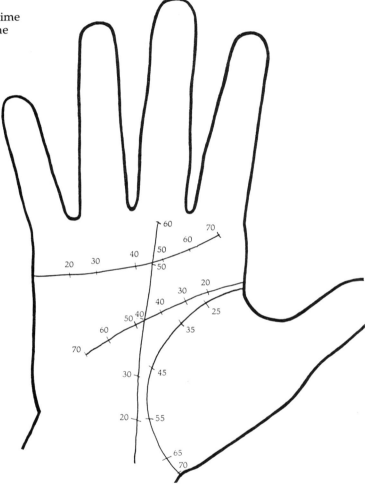

The *life line* is the principal line of the hand. It begins at the edge of the palm between the thumb and Jupiter finger, and arcs downwards around the mount of Venus. Figure 5.11 shows how to gauge time on this and other major lines of the hand.

The life line indicates the strength of our physical constitution and our level of vital force and sexual power. It also records periods of disease, accidents or other life events, some of which can have an impact on our relationships or sexual expression. The life line also indicates *probable* length of life, especially when compared to the length of the other major lines.

Generally speaking, the deeper and stronger the life line, the greater the stamina and sexual energy. Islands on the life line can indicate periods of weak or disturbed sexual energy due to either physical or psychological causes. Any influence lines which cross the life line can produce a similar result, especially if they cause a red or blue dot. A blue or red dot indicates a problem that is physical in origin, such as an illness, accident or operation. When no dot appears where the influence line crosses the life line, the problem is more psychological in origin. Branches on the life line can indicate periods of physical or sexual weakness.

When the life line is long and strong, good health and sexual energy could be enjoyed until old age. When the line becomes weak, the person's energy tends to be low, and interest in sexual activity is reduced.

From a sexual point of view, an 'ideal' life line moves downwards around the mount of Venus in a generous arc, which reveals a strong capacity to love, and a healthy interest in sex. When the line cuts through the mount of Venus, thus limiting its size, there is a tendency towards sexual coldness. When the life line moves towards the mount of Luna, the person would tend to be very restless, and may have difficulty 'settling down' with one person.

THE HEART LINE

The upper transverse line or *heart line* is of special interest to us, because it is our emotional barometer in life. Not only does it reveal the intensity and the quality of our emotions, but it indicates our degree of sensitivity and our capacity for love and affection. It is our primary indicator of the strength, direction and expression of our sexual desire.

The 'ideal' heart line (figure 5.12) is smooth, of good colour, and is relatively free of islands and breaks. It would curve upwards slightly and move across the palm from under the Mercury finger to a point equidistant between the fingers of Jupiter and Saturn, indicating a happy balance between the mind and the emotions. Two or three small branches would appear at its end, revealing a balance between common sense, physical passion, and romantic feelings.

Figure 5.12: The 'ideal' heart line

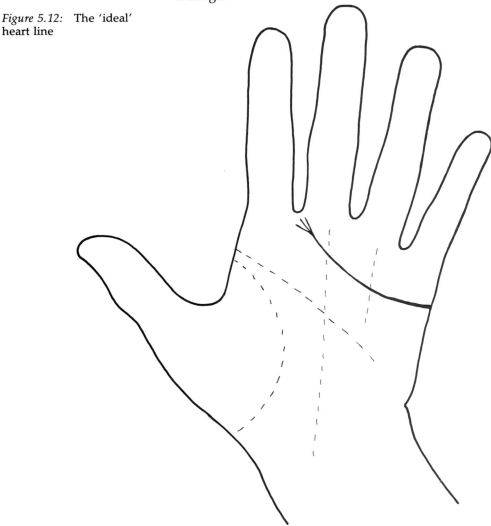

A straight heart line (figure 5.13) reveals a more mental type of lover. Fantasies, images and romance are important aspects of their sexuality, which is primarily receptive in nature. An intimate dinner with champagne, candles and quiet music would be an ideal prelude to passionate sex, which would take place ideally in a comfortable and quiet bedroom with soft music and satin sheets.

Figure 5.13: A straight heart line

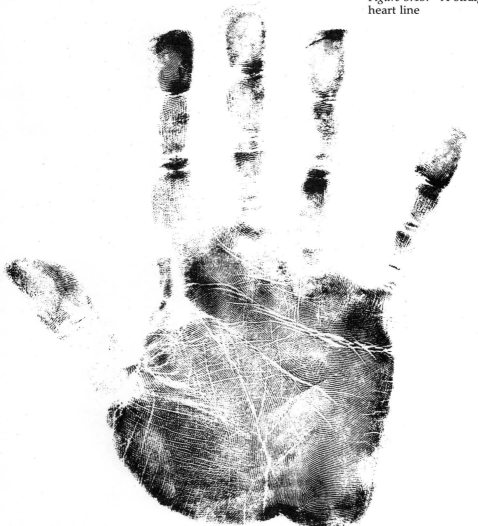

When the heart line curves upwards strongly (figure 5.14) a more physical or instinctual sexuality dominates. People with this type of line prefer more 'rough and tumble' sex like suddenly deciding to make love on the kitchen table, or on the back seat of a car with their clothes on.

Figure 5.14: An upward-curving heart line

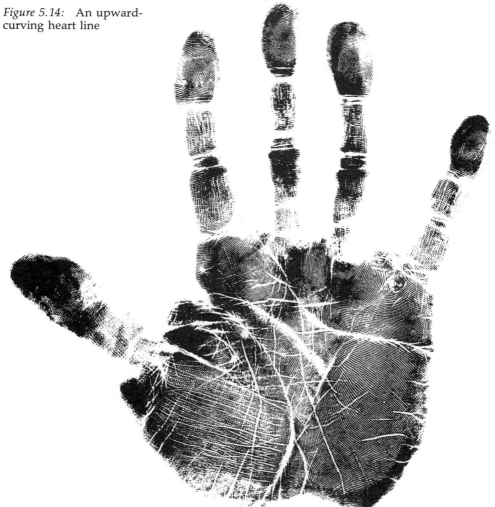

This does not mean that people with mental heart lines would refuse to make love in a Ford or that those with physical heart lines dislike making love in romantic and intimate surroundings. However, the mental and physical heart lines reveal two distinct types of lover who gravitate primarily towards either a mental/receptive or physical/active avenue of sexual expression.

Major characteristics of the heart line include the following:

Ending under Saturn (figure 5.15): Predominantly a physical type of sexuality; run more by the head than by the heart in love relationships; can be emotionally cut off; strong sexual instincts.

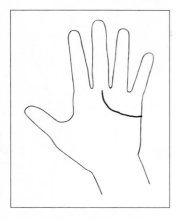

Figure 5.15: Heart line ending under Saturn

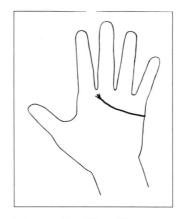

Figure 5.16: Heart line ending between Saturn and Jupiter

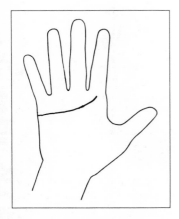

Figure 5.17: Heart line ending under Jupiter

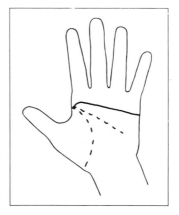

Figure 5.18: Heart line dropping to the head and life lines

Ending between Saturn and Jupiter (figure 5.16) Balance between reason and emotions; warmhearted, generous, sympathetic.

Ending under Jupiter (figure 5.17): Idealistic; ruled more by the heart than the head; more emotional type of sexual urges; a more romantic, poetic and devoted type of lover.

Figure 5.19: A chained heart line

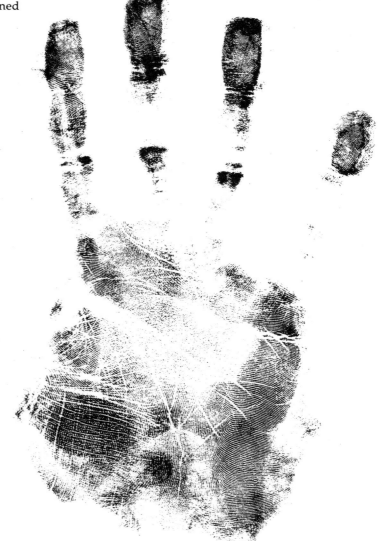

Dropping to the head and life lines (figure 5.18): Strong conflicts between the heart and the head in relationship; powerful emotional feelings; easier to love humanity than individuals.

Chained heart line (figure 5.19): High degree of sensitivity; easily hurt by thoughts and actions of others. Desire for intimate contact, with accompanying fear of commitment; tendency to be promiscuous.

Branches: Receptive nature.

Line joining heart line with head line (figure 5.20): Balance between emotions and intellect in relationships.

Wide space between lines of heart and head (figure 5.21): Broad-minded, unconventional type of mental outlook regarding sex; impulsive and impatient, especially if the lines of life and head are separate. Shares problems and feelings with others.

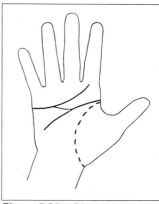

Figure 5.20: Line joining heart line with head line

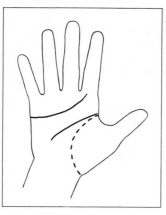

Figure 5.21: Wide space between lines of heart and head

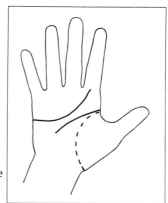

Figure 5.22: Narrow space between heart and head lines

Narrow space between heart and head lines (figure 5.22): Tendency to be afraid, narrow-minded and secretive. Sexually repressed.

THE HEAD LINE

The lower transverse or *head line* begins at the line of life and moves horizontally across the palm. It reveals intelligence, mental capacity, and psychological disposition. It can also show periods of emotional difficulty, worry and mental illness which can affect sexual expression. The head line can reveal any accidents or physical diseases which affect the head as well.

Figure 5.23: Hand print showing long, straight, head line

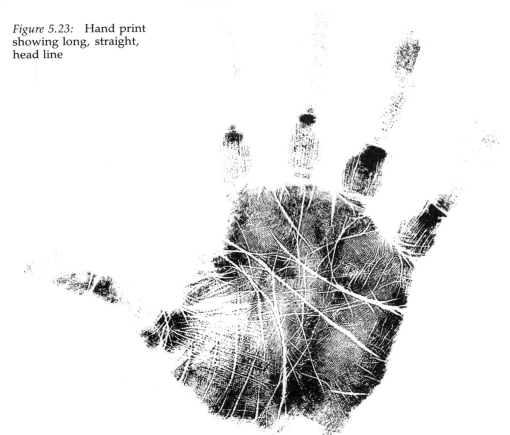

The head line is a reliable indicator of sexual personality. A line that is long and straight (figure 5.23) reveals a practical and realistic person, whose relationships are grounded in reality. On the negative side, however, a person with a straight head line can lack imagination in the bedroom, and would tend to be too devoted to routine and predictable sexual patterns.

To the degree that the headline slopes down towards the mount of Luna (figure 5.24), the imagination plays a stronger role in the person's sexual life. While a person with a sloping head line can be very imaginative in bed, he may also tend to be out of touch with reality when it comes to resolving any difficulties which may be present in the relationship. Be sure to examine other aspects of the hand for confirming or modifying factors.

A head line that contains frets and small islands (figure 5.25) indicates lack of focus and possible inconsistency in relationships. When the islands are large and the head line is broken, there is a potential for deep emotional problems which call for the help of a professional.

When the head line and life line separate at their point of commencement, the individual would tend to be impulsive, impatient and self-reliant in relationships. To the extent that these two lines run together, the greater the caution and dependency. This dependency (which is primarily psychological in nature) can be on one's actual mother and father, or a parent substitute like a lover or spouse. There is also a tendency for the individual to be sexually inhibited and worried about what others may think or say about him.

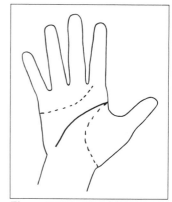

Figure 5.24: Head line plunging towards Luna

THE SIMIAN LINE

The so-called *Simian line* exists when both the heart and head lines join together as one. It appears as a straight line across the hand, as shown in figure 5.26.

The Simian line tends to intensify both the mind and the personality. The individual often alternates between one emotional extreme and the other, with the feelings often in conflict with the intellect. Those who possess this line have great tenacity of purpose and a strong capacity for accomplishment. If the skin texture, mounts and fingers reveal a coarse personality, the owner of the Simian line can be sexually aggressive, angry, violent and unpredictable. Be sure to examine the entire hand before making your evaluation.

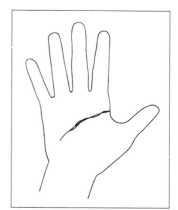

Figure 5.25: 'Islanded' head line

THE SATURN LINE

The line of Saturn or 'line of life task' shows the

degree to which we have fulfilled our deepest goals and our task in life. In the context of our study on sex and relationship, we can note that a weak, broken, wavy or islanded line of Saturn can indicate difficulties in one's career or life path, which in turn can strongly affect the person's relationships. Of course, there are people with highly successful careers and disastrous marriages, and others whose relationships are very fulfilling while their careers are a disappointment. For this reason, it is important to examine both the Saturn line and union line(s) to find any correlations between them.

Figure 5.26: The Simian line

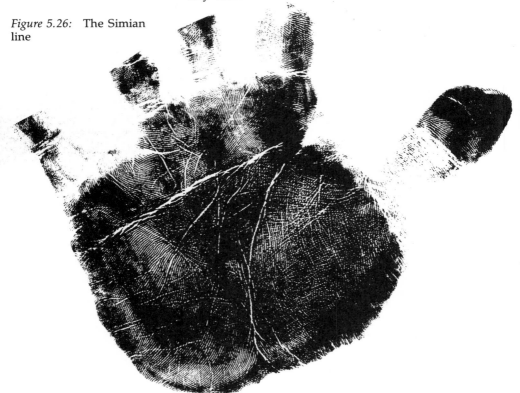

THE MINOR LINES

The *Inner Life Line* provides added strength, vitality and protection to the life line, especially when breaks or islands appear on that line. It also adds to one's potential for enjoying sexual relations, as it indicates a high level of sexual energy.

The *Apollo Line* reveals a love of art and beauty, and is an indicator of creative ability, honours and brilliance. This line can also enhance a person's charm and the ability to feel comfortable in social situations.

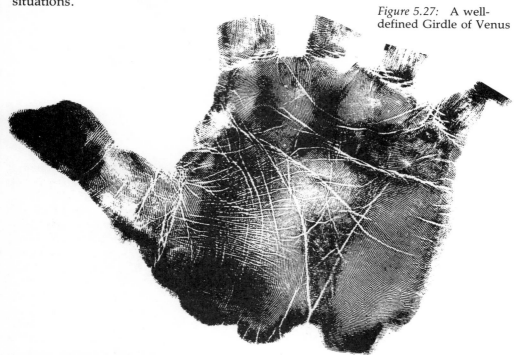

Figure 5.27: A well-defined Girdle of Venus

The *Girdle of Venus* is like a second heart line, and is located between the heart line and the base of the fingers. Altruism, compassion and sexual responsiveness are some of the primary aspects of a girdle of Venus. To the degree that it is clear and well-defined (figure 5.27) the more balanced and properly channelled these emotions will be. However, if the girdle is broken or poorly defined (figure 5.28) the person can be promiscuous, moody and self-indulgent. Examine the entire hand (especially the thumb, heart line, head line and mount of Venus) before arriving at such conclusions, however.

The *Mercury Line* indicates the degree of balance in the physical organism and its basic nervous state. It

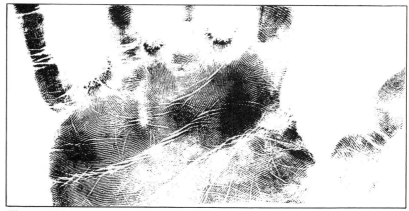

Figure 5.28: A poorly
defined Girdle of Venus

can also reveal potential stomach and intestinal
problems. The line itself has little bearing on sexuality
and relationship, except to the extent that these
maladies can have an impact on one's sex life.

Travel lines reveal journeys of the past, present and
potential future. They are small horizontal lines
located on the outer edge of the palm and move up –
according to the time of the trip in relation to the
person's age – along the mounts of Luna and Mars
towards the heart line. Each line represents an
important journey in terms of distance, duration or
overall impact on the life of the persona involved.
Like the Mercury line, travel lines by themselves have
little to do with the subject of this book. However, to
the degree that frequent travel in the hand of one
partner can have an impact on his relationship, travel
lines *are* important, and must be considered in
conjunction with other lines of the hand.

Lines of Union are small horizontal lines found on
the mount of Mercury and run from the percussion
edge of the hand towards the inside of the palm.
Often known as 'marriage lines', they indicate the
potential for important relationships that impress the
person deeply. While these relationships usually
involve marriage (whether legal or not), they can also
be attachments to other men or women and may or
may not include sex. A more detailed discussion of
the lines of union can be found in chapter 9.

The *Children's Lines* reveal the existence of potential children, especially among women. From my experience, they appear as tiny horizontal lines located beneath the lines of union. Like other aspects of the hand, they reveal *potential* only.

In places like Latin America where contraception and abortion are relatively uncommon, the indication of children on the hand can be fairly accurate. Six children would be represented by six tiny lines under a line of union. In Great Britain, Europe, North America, Australia and other industrialized regions, predicting the number of children is more difficult. Miscarriages and abortions would be recorded as potential children, as well as contraception by artificial means. In general, children's lines can be read with greater accuracy on the hands of women, although they may also exist on the hands of men.

The *Line of Neptune* or 'via lasciva' indicates a strong physical and/or psychological sensitivity to drugs, alcohol, tobacco and other toxic substances, including food additives.

The *Line of Uranus* reveals intuition or psychic ability. An 'ideal' line of Uranus begins in the mount of Luna and moves upwards in a gentle arc towards the mount of Mercury. While this line rarely exists in its pure state, it is often present as a short line (or as a series of short lines) moving diagonally up the mount of Luna. Because its presence indicates a greater degree of intuition and sensitivity, it can reveal a more instinctual individual who should follow his basic hunches in matters of love, sex and relationship.

SECTION II: APPLICATIONS

In the previous section, we examined how the various fingers, mounts, lines and other aspects of the hand can reveal our sexual nature. In the chapters that follow, we will attempt to provide a more comprehensive, integrated and dynamic view of hand characteristics as they relate to our sexual personality and its expression in our relationships with others.

Chapter 6

THE SEXUAL SELF

When we analyse the hands of another person, our primary goal is to achieve a basic 'gestalt' of the individual's psychological essence: the foundation which underlies his or her personality and how it can be expressed in the world. In the context of sexual palmistry, this involves an understanding of the delicate interplay between vital force and its outgrowths, pleasure and aggression. Psychologists say that this dynamic triad makes up the foundation of human sexuality.

In the following pages, we will attempt to examine this relationship between vital force, pleasure and aggression and see how it can be understood and evaluated in the light of both our personality and its expression in the hand.

VITAL FORCE

Albert Szent-Gyorgi, the Nobel-prize-winning physiologist, said that it takes energy to move the wheels of life. This energy virtually impregnates the entire universe, and stands behind all life, creation and evolution on Earth. In humans, this energy (known as *prâna* or *ch'i* in the East) is provided on the physical level by the metabolic processes of the body. This has to do partly with the food we eat, the air we breathe, and our own unique genetic make-up.

In humans, as in other members of the animal kingdom, this *prâna* can be expressed as sexual energy, and is a major motivating force in our lives. However, unlike other animals, the sex force or life force can be channelled into many directions according to our particular circumstances, needs and level of consciousness. On the purely biological level, the sex force stands behind our innate desire to reproduce and further the human species. It impels us to join together with a person of the opposite sex to create a new life.

The *pleasure principle* is strongly connected to our biological instinct for reproduction. According to Alexander Lowen, the 'body's pleasure is the source from which all our good feelings and good thinking stems'. Without pleasure, writes Lowen, one's thinking becomes distorted and creative potential is lost, whether in the creation of a meal, a sculpture or a new life.

Because intimate physical contact with another can be one of the most pleasurable of human experiences, sexual interest is closely related to our ability both to give and to receive pleasure. In the light of our discussion of palmistry and sexuality, evaluating the individual's capacity for pleasure can play an important role in determining sexual interest, direction and functioning.

Aggression is closely linked to both sexual force and the pleasure principle. Although aggression (like pleasure) is often viewed in a negative light, it is essentially *a natural expression of dynamic, outgoing movement vis-à-vis our environment.* It encompasses the self-assertive aspect of the personality, and in its primary expression, serves the function of defence against threats to our vital interests.

When anthropologists speak of aggression in a sexual context, they mention that early *homo sapiens* males (like other male animals) needed to be aggressive in order to subdue, mount and penetrate the female, and thus ensure the continuation of the species. Unfortunately this hold-over 'cave man' mentality has persisted to this day, as evidenced by sexism, rape, paternalist attitudes and other forms of abuse by men against women still prevalent in our culture.

It is important to remember that in palmistry, the triad of sexual energy, pleasure and aggression should not only be considered in the context of a relationship between two people. Depending on our talents, inclinations and level of consciousness, these essentially 'sexual' aspects can be directed in a wide variety of areas. For example, the Shakers (a small celibate utopian Christian community which flourished in the United States during the past century) channelled their sexual energies into creating new and novel forms of art, architecture and furniture design. They are also credited with having made practical improvements on hundreds of inventions and created dozens of new ones, including the clothespin, fountain pen nib, rotary saw, washing machine and flat broom.

This vital force, when properly transmuted, can create at all levels of existence, including those related to art, science and politics. Sexual energy, in conjunction with positive self-assertion and the pleasure principle, can also be channelled towards meditation, devotion and the realization of expanded levels of consciousness. The powers behind healing (including 'therapeutic touch') and the universal expression of peace and goodwill towards all life can spring from this primal sexual force, and incorporate all aspects of the human person.

Therapists have noted that the keys to an integrated sexuality combining sexual energy, pleasure and positive assertion are *awareness* and *intent*. Of course, true awareness comes as a result of our capacity for experiencing real love in our hearts. The sexual force can be channelled towards procreation and starting a family. It can be discharged to bring us pleasure, or to help us release physical and emotional tension. It can be used as a tool to gain power over others, or to increase our belief in our own self-importance. The sexual force can also lead to new levels of intimacy and caring within the context of a relationship, and can create powerful energy forms of love and compassion in the world.

Although our discussion will centre primarily on discovering the potentialities of sexual energy, pleasure and aggression in the hand and how they affect our relationships with others, please bear in mind that non-sexual expressions of these aspects – such as religious devotion, healing and any type of creative endeavour – should be considered as well. The actual expressions of this triad are determined not only by the status of one's present relationship, but also by the individual's primary interests, aspirations and goals.

SEXUAL ENERGY IN THE HAND

Both the thickness and consistency of the hand are major indicators of the amount of sexual energy we have at our disposal. However, other factors, including the size of the mount of Venus and the depth of the life and heart lines, can strengthen or neutralize these basic characteristics. While the thickness of the hand is partly determined by physique, a very flat and soft hand with a prominent indentation in the centre of the open palm reveals a very low sex drive. A person with this type of hand – especially if it is pale – would tend to tire easily, lack warmth, and probably be somewhat 'needy' in a relationship: he would rather be 'given to' than give. A person with this kind of thin, soft hand often lacks the warmth of heart so necessary to a deep relationship, and will tend to intellectualize his feelings and stay aloof from emotional confront- ations, especially if the fingers are long and knotted and the line of heart is long and chained. However, if the hand is thin and hard, the person can be stubborn, inflexible and calculating as well. If the thumb is stiff and the head and heart lines join at their commencement, the individual would tend to withhold from others on both emotional and sexual levels.

A thick, fleshy hand reveals the opposite qualities: an abundance of warmth (both physical and emotional), high energy and powerful sensuality. When the hand is thick and soft, chances are that the person loves food and drink almost as much as sex. Weight control can be a problem.

A hand of medium thickness – in both women and men – reflects a person with a moderate degree of energy and warmth. Like attitudes towards food and drink, their sexual appetites are generally balanced. They tend not to be disinterested in sex, but it isn't an all-consuming passion unless mitigating factors are present, such as a very large mount of Venus.

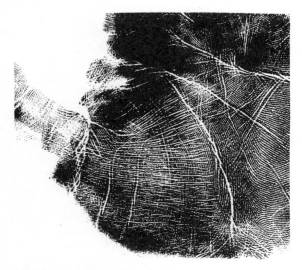

Figure 6.1: A well-formed mount of Venus

As our primary indicator of passion and sex drive, the mount of Venus speaks of vitality, the capacity for friendship, and the ability to love. Ideally, it should occupy about one-third of the palmar surface, and be bordered by a life line forming a graceful arc towards the wrist (as seen in figure 6.1). Being neither too

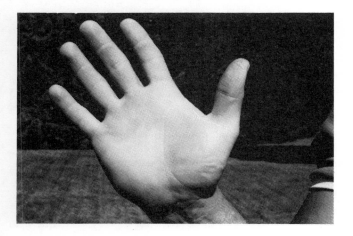

Figure 6.2: A very large mount of Venus

hard nor too bland, 'nice and round and cushy' would best describe a good mount of Venus. When healthy pink in colour and free of deep grilles, it reflects vitality, warmth and energy, revealing a strong capacity to love and be loved in return. If the mount is very large (figure 6.2), there is a potential for an over-abundance of physical passion and sexuality. Unless a strong head line and thumb are present, the pursuit of sexual gratification can run much of the person's life. Unless blessed with a partner who is also highly sexed, strenuous physical activities like jogging, chopping wood or raquetball should be pursued so that this abundant sexual energy is channelled elsewhere.

However, if the mount is flat and soft, there may be a lack of vitality and sexual power. Although the individual can be capable of strong feelings of love and passion, they may not be expressed primarily in the bedroom. If the life line cuts into this mount rather than sweeping around it in a wide arc (figure 6.3) the person can often be cold, Victorian and prudish. Sexual expression is not a priority in life.

Figure 6.3: A mount of Venus cut by the life line

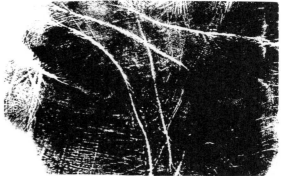

Another indicator of sexual energy is the colour of the nails. Those with reddish nails tend to possess a strong sex drive and are more able to express this passion in purely physical terms. Bright pink nails tend to modify this powerful sex drive somewhat, and their owners are more likely to enjoy more of a balance between the physical and emotional expressions of love and passion. People with bluish nails often have difficulty expressing themselves physically. Although they do not necessarily lack passion and strong feelings of sexual love, it often takes them some time to 'warm up' to another person, especially if their hands reveal a tendency towards introversion and shyness.

PLEASURE

Like other aspects of the personality, the hand can reveal only our *potential* for receiving and enjoying pleasure. Unless mitigating factors are present in life, a person with a thick, soft and fleshy hand of moderate consistency, with short, smooth fingers and fine, pinkish skin would probably be a pleasure-loving individual, as these traits would point to a highly sensuous being who relates to others in a physical way. In addition to good food and soft pillows, frequent physical contact with others would rank high among the joys of life. A deep and slightly chained heart line (which can both increase sensitivity and emotional depth) can accentuate these inclinations, as would a prominent mount of Venus, a large mount of the Moon, pink nails, and conic or spatulate fingertips. This would be especially true if the hand and thumb are flexible, because they can increase one's ability to respond to inner feelings and primal instincts without being held back by outer rules imposed by society or parents.

On the opposite end of the scale, people with thin, bony hands, a small or restricted mount of Venus, cold skin temperature, long, knotted fingers, bluish or pale nails and weak lines would not consider sensate pleasure as a priority in life. The idea of a quiet Sunday of church, conversation, reading a book, and afternoon tea, would probably interest them more than an active morning of love-making, a late and abundant brunch, and another afternoon tryst lasting until the evening.

There are, of course, numerous modifying characteristics in the hand which can indicate a greater or diminished capacity for physical pleasure. The position of the thumb on the hand, the basic shape of the hand, and the presence of a girdle of Venus, for example, can offer important information that can modify other attributes. These and other hand characteristics will be discussed in detail in the following chapter.

SEXUAL AGGRESSION

As we mentioned before, the aggressive instinct of early *homo sapiens* helped ensure the survival of the species. It not only protected early women and men from the dangers of an often hostile environment, but encouraged them to bond together for the purpose of procreation. Although much has changed over the course of human history, modern men and women still carry this primal instinct to bond sexually with another human being. While fortunately this aggressive instinct does not always manifest itself as a violent or forceful imposition of one's personal will over another for sexual gratification, it generally takes the form of a more benign and positive self-assertion and a natural desire for affection, intimacy and sexual contact with another human being.

As in determining the amount of sexual energy, the firmer the consistency of the hand the more assertive the personality. This can be strengthened by a long, firm thumb, a firm or stiff hand which barely bends back under pressure, reddish nails and reddish skin, as opposed to pale nails and skin. While a large mount of Venus can be a reliable indicator of strong sexual interest, a large mount that is also hard can increase the potential for sexual aggressiveness, especially if the mount is reddish in colour. Strong grilles on this mount (as opposed to fine lines) accentuate physical passion and the strong desire to achieve rapid sexual release.

A large and well-formed mount of lower Mars reveals a strong desire to satisfy sexual urges. While a relatively soft and nicely rounded mount would show a healthy degree of sexual self-assertion, a prominent, hard and reddish mount (it almost appears to be a callous) reveals strong currents of aggression which could spill over into cruelty and violence. When these traits are accompanied by what hand readers call a 'murderer's thumb' (consult chapter 3) the person is capable of losing control and can be a real danger to others, especially if the other fingers of the hand are bent in any way.

We mentioned earlier that the presence of a Simian line can increase emotional intensity. Unless modified by other aspects of the hand, the owner of a Simian line can alternate from one emotional extreme to another without warning. Loving and affectionate one moment, he can be angry and aggressive the next. An hour later, all anger will be forgotten. The potential for aggression and cruelty is especially strong if the skin texture and hand are coarse in appearance (figure 6.4), as opposed to the more sensitive hand shown in figure 6.5. The tendency towards callousness and violence can sometimes be offset, however, by markings of sensitivity including obvious pads on the fingertips, a chained or fretted Simian line, and the presence of a girdle of Venus. Be sure to examine the entire hand carefully before arriving at any firm conclusions.

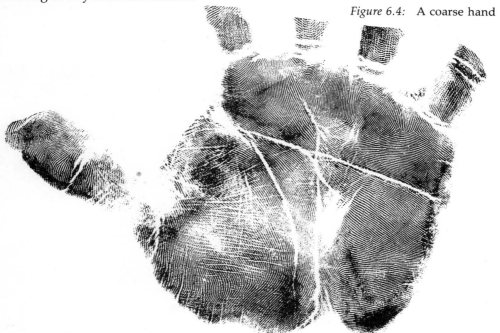

Figure 6.4:   A coarse hand

Frequently, people whose Jupiter finger is larger than the Apollo like to dominate and exercise control over others in social situations. If the mounts of Venus and Mars are small and relatively soft, the desire for control would be essentially benign. However, if a strong Jupiter finger is accompanied by prominent or hard mounts of Mars and Venus, the individual would tend to be aggressive and pushy. There will be a clear effort to 'be on top' in a relationship, especially if the hand, thumb and other fingers are stiff and inflexible. If the life and head lines separate at their commencement, these strong assertive tendencies are an essential component of the individual's natural personality. However, if these lines are joined, the desire to dominate and control stems primarily from a basic insecurity which says 'If I am not in charge in this relationship, my partner will dominate over me.' The person can be aggressive and pushy as a result, as he strives to achieve and maintain control over the partner.

Figure 6.5: A sensitive hand

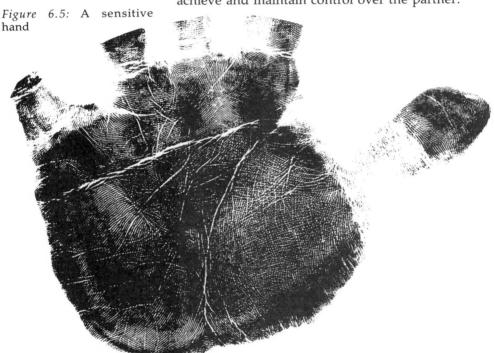

Sexual aggression can also be indicated by the heart line. If the line is more of the 'physical' type, the person tends to be sexually more aggressive and enjoys 'rough and tumble' sex. This is especially true if the line lacks frets, chains or islands. Romance, flowers and soft words of affection would tend to be favoured by the person with the 'mental' heart line. While there may be an abundance of love and passion, it will probably be expressed more through the heart rather than through the genitals. For this reason, people with this type of heart line often need to be more sexually assertive in their relationships in order to achieve a greater sense of mutuality with their partner.

With care and experience, it will not be difficult for the hand analyst to achieve a well-grounded understanding of this triad of sexual energy, pleasure and aggression and how they help determine the psychosexual personality of the person we are reading for. In the following chapter, we will continue onwards from this foundation, and explore the major psychological issues involving sex and relationship and how they can be seen in the hand.

Chapter 7

PERSONALITY TRAITS AND SEXUAL EXPRESSION

There are numerous factors which contribute to our sexual personality. In addition to the essential anatomical and physical appearance we inherit from our parents, we also receive physiological and hormonal characteristics which govern body metabolism and our physical reactions to the world around us. We also come into the world with a basic constitutional disposition, which governs our energy level and the ability to respond to challenges from our environment.

Aside from physical characteristics like appearance and size, we also inherit psychological traits from our mother and father. Like the genes involved with physical processes like circulation, digestion and reproduction, our mental and emotional functions are often strongly imprinted with the genes of our parents. A statement like 'You think just like your father' is not only based on psychological conditioning (which is in itself considerable) but also on inherited genetic traits. This is why in many cases, the hands of parents and their children can have much in common.

Environmental factors also play a role in psychosexual development. Pre-natal, natal and post-natal traumas of either physical or psychological origin, primary emotional and physical reactions to one's mother and father, and the child's relationships with brothers and sisters during the first years of life often influence the way we relate to other people and the world around us. Other childhood traumas, such as the loss of a close relative or friend, a chronically poor family situation, or the more serious (and often overlooked) problem of sexual abuse by elders can also contribute strongly to psychosexual development. In addition, cultural influences from family, friends, school, church and the media all condition us to adapt to 'acceptable' standards of society. Teaching a boy that 'real men don't cry' or that a girl should play with dolls and avoid active sports are but two of the more obvious examples of this kind of societal influence which helps mould our psychosexual nature.

In the pages that follow, we will examine some major psychological traits, how they can be seen in the hand, and how they can be applied to a psychosexual hand analysis. As mentioned before, the hand reveals tendencies and predispositions, and the lines can change over time. In addition, it is important for the hand reader to consider several hand characteristics together before making a final evaluation. In many cases, an indicator from one hand characteristic can contradict that of another. For this reason, it is wise to proceed with care and strive to achieve a *whole view* of the hands before arriving at any firm conclusions regarding the psychological and sexual make-up of the person we are reading for.

ROMANTIC/REALISTIC

You can spot a romantic person by his intensity. When he falls in love, it is instinctual and often 'at first sight'. His relationships are often deeply emotional with a powerful sensual component. Sex tends to be varied, stimulating and frequent.

The major indication of a romantic is the heart line. It would be deep, long and extend well into the mount of Jupiter. Chances are that the heart line would be of the 'mental' variety, which will increase one's emotional sensitivity and impressionability. Conic or psychic fingertips (especially on the Jupiter finger) tend to strengthen romantic and devotional tendencies, as does a large mount of Venus, which reveals deep passion. The presence of a girdle of Venus may also indicate a tendency towards romanticism, especially when it accompanies the 'mental' heart line described above. In addition, the head line of a pure romantic would probably droop down towards the mount of Luna, increasing the strength of the imagination as well as the tendency to dream.

Hands of the realist tend to be more squarish, and feature square or spatulate fingertips. The palmar surface is broad as opposed to narrow (narrow, elongated hands appear to be more common among romantics) and the head line – which is probably clear and long – moves straight across the palm towards the mount of Upper Mars. Unlike the romantic, the realist's heart line tends more towards the 'physical' type, and ends either at the mount of Saturn or just beyond. It is important to remember that many romantic individuals try to appear to others as realistic, despite their long, chained or broken heart lines. This duality would be especially true if the hand is squarish and the head line practical.

Disillusionment is a common event in the life of romantics. They often place the object of their desire on a pedestal and expect more than can realistically be given. The tendency to overestimate others is found when the Apollo finger bends towards Saturn. If the Apollo finger is straight, one's primary instinct about another person is usually correct, especially if the person's hand features lines of intuition moving upwards from the mount of Luna. However, whether or not these basic hunches are followed is another story!

A Mercury finger which curves slightly towards Apollo denotes an astute individual who is not easily deceived by others. When this finger is perfectly straight, the owner may be too trusting or naive. Though trusting others is an admirable quality, it can often lead to disappointment in a relationship, especially if the individual is a poor judge of other people and their motives.

COMMUNICATION

The ability to communicate with another person is essential for relationship. In palmistry, a long Mercury finger (i.e. which reaches at least to the top phalange of the Apollo finger) is a primary indicator of communicating ability. Often found in the hands of writers, actors, teachers and public speakers, a long Mercury finger enables one to be comfortable with others in social situations, and reveals an innate ability to share one's thoughts and feelings with little or no difficulty.

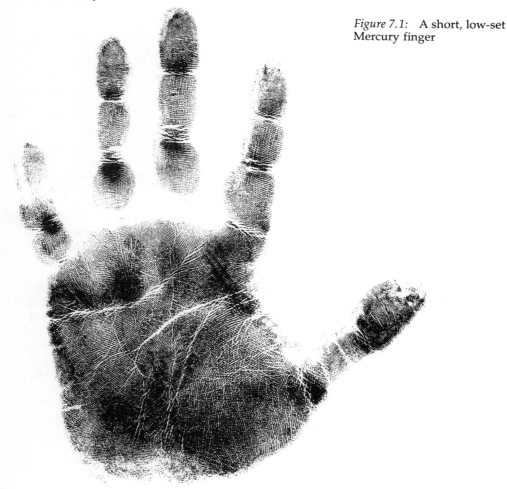

Figure 7.1: A short, low-set Mercury finger

By the same token, a short Mercury finger that is low-set in the hand (as seen in figure 7.1) reduces one's ability to communicate. The person feels ill at ease in social situations, and is easily misunderstood by others. However, a strong, well-formed Apollo finger (especially if it has a spatulate tip) will enhance the ability to communicate.

To the extent that the Mercury finger curves towards Apollo, the person tends to be astute and shrewd in relationships. People who are especially charming and seductive (sexually or otherwise) often have this type of finger. A popular South American president, nicknamed 'The Silver Haired Fox' by both friends and opponents alike, reportedly had a long, curving Mercury finger. Despite his poor record as a leader, he was able to charm himself out of even the most damaging political situations through his uncanny ability to communicate.

A wide separation between the lines of heart and head (figure 7.2) tends to reveal a person who wants to share his thoughts and feelings with others. This openness is enhanced by fingers which are widely spaced (especially when the hand is held open), a low-set thumb, and head and life lines which are separate at their commencement. A narrow space between the heart and head lines (figure 7.3) is a good indication of a secretive person who prefers to keep his feelings and opinions to himself. Of course, if you want to share a secret with someone, the owner of this type of line configuration would be ideal, especially if his hand is firm or rigid.

During a hand analysis, one can sometimes find a subject with a narrow space between the heart and head lines, the life and head lines joined at their commencement, and a strongly curving Saturn finger, which indicates a tendency towards depression. Sometime an imaginative head line is present as well. In this case, when the person becomes depressed, his imagination often makes a small problem into a major tragedy. At the same time, the person's secretive nature will prevent him from sharing his difficulty with another, thus robbing him of the opportunity for feedback, sympathy or comfort.

Since communication involves receiving as well as sharing, the degree of open-mindedness is an

Figure 7.2: A wide separation between heart and head lines

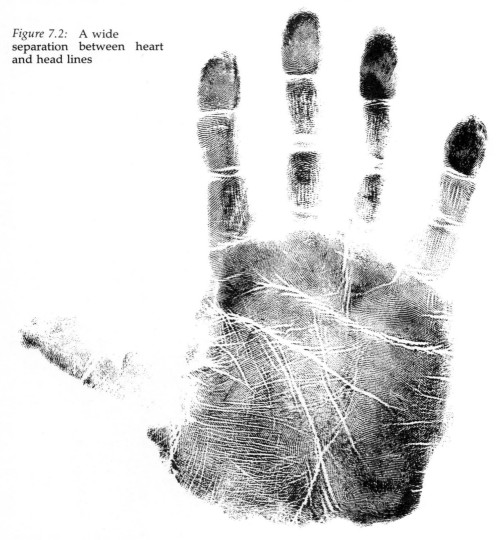

important aspect of communication. Generally speaking, people with broad hands, a low-set thumb and large, broad nails, are psychologically open and easy to talk to. They are often interested in other points of view and are tolerant of the feelings of others. A chained or fretted heart line (especially if it is long) will reveal a person who is sensitive to other people and who cares about their problems.

When the palm is narrow or elongated, however, the person tends to be more conservative and closed-minded, especially if the hand is firm or rigid. Short nails (which have not been bitten) reveal a critical person who may tend to be negative and bigoted towards other people's points of view.

Figure 7.3: A narrow separation between heart and head lines

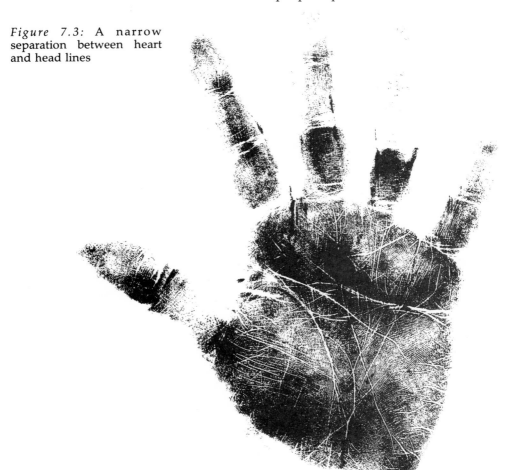

EXTROVERSION, INTROVERSION AND SEXUAL INHIBITION

Studies have shown that the sex lives of extroverts

and introverts differ substantially. Extroverts, who are less inhibited than introverts, generally have their first sexual experience at an earlier age, and enjoy a more active sex life through adulthood. They are likely to experiment with more sexual partners, explore a greater variety of sexual techniques, and (among females at least) experience orgasm more frequently than those who are introverted.

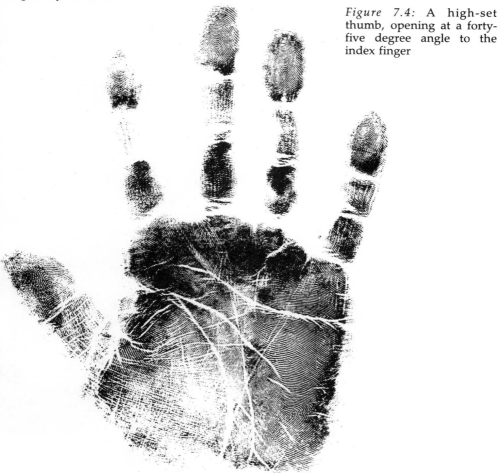

Figure 7.4: A high-set thumb, opening at a forty-five degree angle to the index finger

When analysing a person's hand, ask them to open both hands as far as comfortably possible. Pay special attention to the thumb. The greater the degree formed between the index finger and the open thumb, the greater the degree of extroversion and sexual liberation.

A high-set thumb, opening at a forty-five-degree angle to the index finger (figure 7.4) is a sign of a Victorian in sexual attitudes. The person is overly cautious, correct and withdrawn sexually, and is often embarrassed about sexual matters to the point

Figure 7.5: A low-set, wide-angled thumb

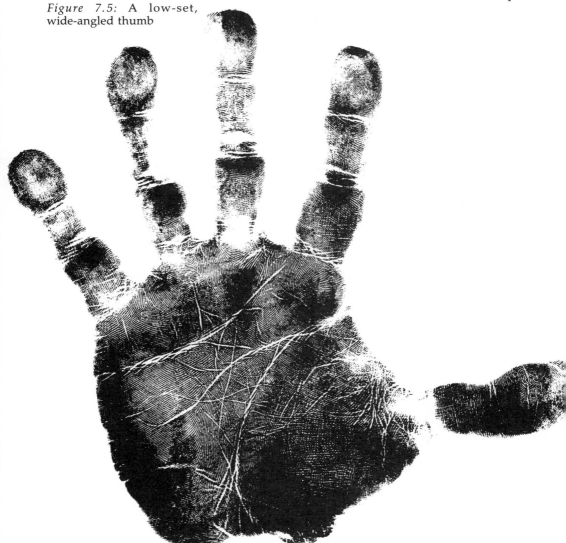

of avoiding them completely. Such an individual would tend to be very cautious in a relationship and would have difficulty 'letting go'. In popular jargon, he would be best described as 'uptight' unless modifying aspects in the hand are present.

When the thumb is set at a sixty-degree angle, there is a greater degree of psychological openness. While more sexually liberated than the Victorian, there is still a fear of letting go in an emotional or sexual sense, and flowing with the movement of life.

A low-set thumb (figure 7.5) can be positioned at a ninety-degree angle to the Jupiter finger. People with low-set thumbs tend to be more self-accepting and sexually integrated than others. They are generally more adaptable, more versatile and have a greater ability to 'hang loose' in a relationship than others. Because they are often more independent than most people, there is a corresponding interest in sexual adventure and experimentation.

There are several important modifiers to consider when examining the degree of the thumb. Spatulate or conic fingers, a 'generous' thumb, and a flexible hand tend to increase extroversion, while stiff hands, squarish fingertips, and a 'stubborn' thumb tend to increase self-control and sexual repression. A separation of the head and life lines at their commencement tends to reveal a person who is more impulsive, impatient and self-reliant, thus decreasing sexual inhibition and self-restraint. Knotted fingers can enhance sexual inhibition. They are found mostly on people who analyse and who focus on minutiae, especially if their fingers are long. If the fingers tend to be held closely together when the hand is opened, the underlying psychological insecurity of the individual can also manifest as repression and inhibition in their sexual lives. A hand with widely spread fingers would tend to reveal a person who is not sexually inhibited or repressed.

Some people possess a small but obvious horizontal line which moves across the mount of Luna (figure 7.6). Although it can be confused with a travel line, I have found this line especially on people's hands who love adventure and risk. Whether this love of adventure will carry over to one's romantic life can be seen by observing the features of the entire hand.

91

Figure 7.6: A line on the mount of Luna denoting a love of adventure

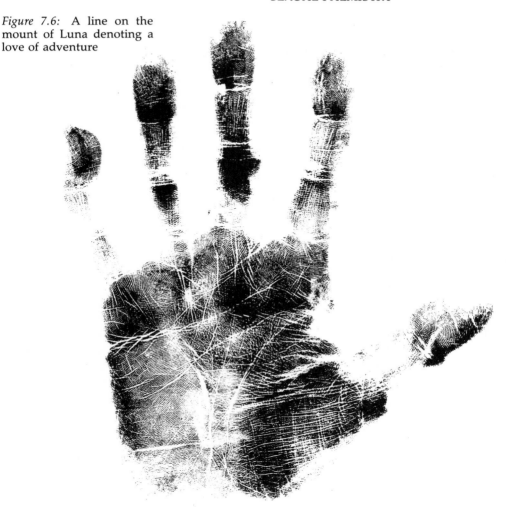

SELF-ESTEEM

Our level of self-esteem plays an important role in our sexual lives. Because people with a high degree of self-esteem like themselves better, they tend to attract both people and situations which enhance their lives. As a result, they are more able to realize their fondest dreams whether in business, sports or relationships.

Like other aspects of the personality, our level of self-esteem is determined partly by inherited factors with which we come into the world, along with childhood conditioning from parents, school and religious training. For this reason, it is important for the reader to consider both hands when doing an analysis in order to learn if the degree of self-esteem has increased over the years, has decreased, or has remained the same since early childhood.

The major indicators of self-esteem in the hand include the Jupiter finger, the Apollo finger, and the relationship of the life line to the head line at their commencement. Ideally, the two fingers should be of equal length, indicating a good amount of self-esteem and a realistic vision of one's innate strengths and weaknesses. To the degree that the Jupiter finger is shorter than Apollo, the lower the basic level of self-esteem. When this exists, there is a tendency not to give oneself the credit due, and to underestimate many qualities which one may, in fact, possess. In relationship, low self-esteem can sometimes lead a person to become involved in romantic or sexual situations in the hope of improving his self-image.

A long Jupiter finger (especially if it is strong) would indicate a greater innate level of self-esteem, especially if the lines of head and life are separate at their commencement. Such a combination reveals a high degree of self-love and self-acceptance, which can translate into self-confidence and the ability to take risks in a relationship. The joining of the life and head lines betrays insecurity and caution. This can, in turn, open the door to vanity, pride and exaggerated feelings of self-importance that are based more on underlying feelings of insecurity than on inner strength.

As mentioned before, early childhood trauma can seriously erode our inherited level of self-esteem. We can often locate such trauma (whether it is physical, psychological or both) by observing where influence lines cross the life, head and heart lines. A physical trauma (such as an accident or serious illness) will often leave a small red or bluish dot on the line when crossed by the influence line, while a psychological trauma would probably be free of such dots. To the extent that the influence line breaks or causes an island to form on a major line, the greater the impact and/or duration of the psychological or physical trauma. It is important to remember, however, that not all traumas necessarily erode self-esteem. In some cases, a major accident or other trauma can have a powerful healing effect on the personality and lead a person to feel better about themselves than before.

Frequently our level of self-esteem can have an important impact on how we view our partners and our relationships with them. Jealousy is one of the most common results of low self-esteem and often needs to be recognized and dealt with constantly. Jealousy can be seen in the hand by the Jupiter finger curving towards Saturn. The greater the curve, (as long as it is not due to arthritis or accident), the more innately jealous and . possessive the individual. Conversely, a relatively straight Jupiter finger would reveal a more open person who doesn't treat his partner like private property that can be taken away by a rival.

FAITHFULNESS

Unfortunately, there is no sure indication for faithfulness in the hand. However, a strong thumb and firm-to-rigid hand, squarish fingers and a relatively clear heart line ending under the mount of Jupiter would enhance the qualities of responsibility, reliability and loyalty towards another person. In many cases, this sense of loyalty is not wholly dependent on sexual satisfaction, as sex is usually neither more nor less important than other aspects of the relationship.

Very flexible hands, a 'generous' thumb, and separate life and head lines tend to indicate a more spontaneous (and often less reliable) individual, especially if the head line is islanded and the upper mount of Mars is soft, indicating lack of persistence and possible commitment. If the heart line is very long and chained, the person can be interested sexually in a wide variety of partners, and find it difficult to be completely devoted to one. By the same token, a person with a heart line ending under the Saturn mount, would be more interested in sexual pleasure than loyalty to his mate. The tendency for promiscuity is enhanced by a girdle of Venus (especially if it is broken) and an abnormally large Venus mount, indicating that interest in sex (and sexual satisfaction) is a primary goal in life. Another sign of potential promiscuity is a low-set Mercury finger. According to the respected Australian palmist Andrew Fitzherbert, a person with this trait has difficulty finding satisfaction in their relationship, and will tend to 'shop around' for the ideal partner.

GENEROSITY

Generosity is among the finest of human virtues, and can be found in all happy long-term relationships. These days, generosity without imposing conditions is rare, and the person who freely gives and expects nothing in return is considered an anomaly.

The primary indicator for generosity is the flexible thumb, as shown in figure 7.7. The more the thumb bends back, the more inherently generous the individual, whether with money, possessions or affection. Generosity is enhanced by a flexible hand which is fairly soft in consistency. A flabby upper mount of Mars can indicate difficulty resisting outside pressures, so a person with a generous thumb and a soft mount of upper Mars often has difficulty saying 'no' to others. A stronger overall hand and a firm mount can temper this tendency somewhat and lead to more discrimination.

The less flexible the thumb, the more circumspect and wilful the individual. He may be very generous to certain people, but would probably not be generous to all. In general, the more rigid the hand and thumb, the more inherently withholding the owner on both material and emotional levels.

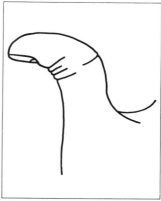

Figure 7.7:   Flexible thumb

SENSITIVITY

One's degree of sensitivity can be detected primarily

Figure 7.8:   A chained heart line with girdle of Venus

by the texture of the skin. As pointed out in chapter 2, the finer the skin, the more emotionally (and physically) sensitive the individual. A profusion of lines, in addition to fine skin will enhance sensitivity, especially if the heart line is long and chained and accompanied by a girdle of Venus, as seen in figure 7.8. Generally speaking, women tend to have a finer skin texture than men, but this is not always the case.

Another sign of sensitivity are tiny pads on the tips of the fingers, which often resemble small tumours. They not only reveal tactile sensitivity, but emotional impressionability as well.

DOMINANT/SUBMISSIVE

Like issues of assertiveness and passivity, sexual dominance and submission are often difficult to read in the hand. In classical palmistry it is taught that assertive and dominant people would tend to have long, strong and low-set thumbs, a long or strong Jupiter finger, life and head lines separated at their commencement, a clear head line (revealing mental focus and clarity), a firm and somewhat inflexible hand (betraying stubbornness and strength of character), and strong mounts of Jupiter (revealing leadership) and Mars (indicating assertiveness). A stereotype 'passive' individual would possess the opposite hand characteristics: a short, weak, high-set thumb, a weak or short Jupiter finger, a soft mount of Mars, and so on.

However, classic palmists often overlooked the fact that strong currents of domination and submission (or assertiveness and passivity) are normally found in the same person and can change according to a particular relationship or situation the person is involved in at the time. It has been found that many tough military men and cut-throat business executives who are extremely dominating towards their peers and subordinates like to be passive and even submissive with their sexual partners.

Supposedly 'passive' individuals often release their aggression when the right opportunity presents itself. For this reason, the hand reader must be very sensitive to all aspects of the hand and take often contradictory characteristics into account when forming a basic impression of the person whose hands are being analysed. Is the person naturally dominant, or is 'taking charge' used to compensate for a fear of being dominated by others? Is the individual submissive by nature, or is he merely holding in his assertive qualities for fear that he may lose control, or be disliked by others if he acts them out?

FANTASY

Fantasy is a major component of our psychosexual make-up. In addition to physical stimulation, mental stimulation is essential for sexual arousal and functioning. Depending on how we understand (and hopefully learn from) our fantasies, we can not only enhance the quality of our relationships, but increase our level of self-understanding as well.

Sexual fantasies can take three major forms. The first (and most common) type of fantasy takes the form of an escape from a boring, humdrum existence. The overworked housewife who dreams about being kidnapped by a handsome prince on a white horse entertains this type of fantasy. Based on sales of gothic romance novels among women (and the popularity of magazines like *Playboy* and *Penthouse* among men) this 'escape' type of fantasy is perhaps the most widespread of all.

The second category of fantasies are of a deeply personal nature which often involve an unfulfilled desire or longing towards a specific person. A man who has sexual fantasies about his wife's sister, or a woman who fantasizes about having an affair with her gardener are two such examples. In many cases, such fantasies can be used to help one understand and come to terms with a problem in life that can be resolved within the context of the existing relationship or with the help of short-term therapy. Whether this type of fantasy is shared with the partner, left alone or acted upon depends on the situation.

The third fantasy category is of the 'deviant' variety, which may involve violence, humiliation, exhibitionism or suffering. Far more serious than mere escape, such fantasies often go back to deep psychological traumas from childhood. Because of strong feelings of guilt or shame which often

97

accompany such fantasies, they are often kept a secret, which may lead them to be occasionally acted out in real life at a tremendous personal cost.

Since everyone experiences fantasies of various kinds and intensities at one time or another (psychologists claim that the average adult has a sexual fantasy every three minutes) a palmist shouldn't make generalities regarding a 'fantasy-prone' hand.

Nevertheless, there are a number of aspects in the hand which reveal that imagination and fantasy play

Figure 7.9: A head line dropping towards the mount of Luna

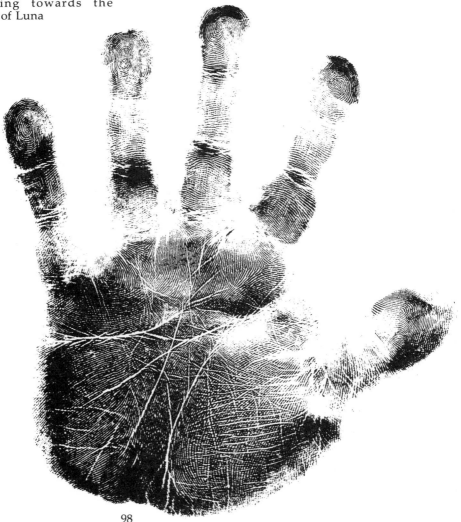

98

a major role in one's life. Whether this potential is channelled into writing a science fiction novel or creating a bizarre sexual scenario can be seen by examining the entire hand carefully, and being aware of the variety of messages the hand and its markings can offer.

Generally speaking, a head line which drops towards the mount of Luna (figure 7.9) would indicate a rich fantasy life as opposed to a 'realistic' head line which moves straight across the palm. If the line is clear and long, the sexual fantasies can be interesting and varied, although the fantasizer would still be grounded in the reality of the 'here and now'. However, a head line that is broken, weak or islanded, or a skin texture which features a 'string of pearls' (see page 29) indicate that neurotic tendencies may be present and the person may have difficulty distinguishing between fantasy and reality. Associating characteristics which point in the direction of unreality can include a weak thumb, a flexible hand, and fingers which are conic, psychic or severely bent (especially the fingers of Saturn and Apollo). If these features are accompanied by a long, chained and deep heart line and a large mount of Venus, one's fantasy life can actually have a detrimental influence on one's relationships. In such rare cases, the individual can live in a genuine fantasy world and be out of touch with reality.

When evaluating the potential for fantasy in the hand, be sure to examine all aspects of both hands in order to obtain a balanced and integrated view of the person. What is the degree of sexual inhibition? Is the person basically sensitive or insensitive to others? What impact might an unhappy career or relationship have on the person's fantasy life? Generally speaking, a person's sexual fantasies need not be considered a problem unless they are disrupting his personal life and threaten his relationship with others.

In many cases, the sharing of sexual fantasies with others and trying to understand their message can be very useful. However, it is important to remember that the vast majority of hand readers are not sex therapists and should not attempt to do sexual counselling. Clients should be referred to a qualified professional rather than attempting to offer therapy yourself.

Chapter 8

SEXUAL VARIETIES, SEXUAL CHOICES

We mentioned before that sexual expression has its roots in our basic genetic make-up, educational, cultural and religious conditioning, and especially our primary relationships with our mother and father. For those who believe in reincarnation, experiences and lifestyles from previous incarnations are also said to have a major impact on our sexuality in our present life. Each sexual relationship mobilizes different aspects of this reality in us. For this reason, it is important to consider sexual expression as part of our *overall being* rather than as a separate compartment in life.

When it comes to dealing with unconventional styles of sexual behaviour, books on palmistry generally tend to ignore the larger issues involved, or discuss unorthodox sexual expression with strong moralistic overtones. This is clearly not helpful to the person who comes to the palmist for assistance, because an important and intimate part of his/her life is being judged, sensationalized or placed in a trivial light by another. For this reason, hand readers should try to be as objective as possible when examining an individual's sexual personality, and be aware of our own personal fears, prejudices and conditioning. We must also be wary about making broad statements about the worth or value of another person's sexual style, especially if it involves behaviour we do not understand or have never experienced.

This does not mean that we should avoid being honest and direct when we share information with the person whose hands we are reading. However, given the seriousness of the subject – as well as the needs of those who seek our help – we should approach issues of unconventional sexual expression with sensitivity and respect.

MASTURBATION

Masturbation is an almost universal phenomenon among human beings throughout the world. It is so widespread, sexologists believe that we can hardly speak of it as 'unconventional'. For those interested in the origins of words, masturbation appears to be a corruption of the latin *manu stuprare* or 'to defile with the hand'.

In years past, 'touching yourself' was viewed with horror, and was considered an act so vile in the sixteenth and seventeenth centuries that only veiled references to it were accepted in polite company. Even in the early part of this century, 'scientific' books of the day claimed that masturbation was responsible for 'tapping the very fountains of neuro-vitality, and drains from the blood all its purest and most strengthening qualities' and could lead to a variety of diseases including 'neurathemia, mental depression and insanity'.*

Like public opinion of the time, many books on palmistry taught that masturbation was both perverted and sinful, and reported that people who practise 'self-abuse' could be identified (to their shame) by a sweaty palm, blotches on the back of the hands, or a large red grille on the mount of Venus.

Although sexual self-stimulation is viewed in a more enlightened frame of reference, it still produces a good deal of misunderstanding, which is not only restricted to teenage boys who are worried about

* *Dr Foote's New Book on Health and Disease*, New York, 1903.

losing their teeth or developing hairy palms. It should be of concern to the hand reader only if sexual guilt – which stems primarily from old moralistic views – and sexual repression seem to be a major problem for the person whose hands we are reading.

At the present time, psychologists consider masturbation to have several positive and even therapeutic aspects. It can be used as a way to discharge sexual energy and relieve tension when an appropriate sexual partner is not available. In addition, auto-erotic activity can be used to bring us into deeper contact with our body and its sensations. Many women, and also men, practise masturbation this way in order to later achieve more fulfilling sexual relations with their partner.

Another, perhaps more controversial view of the therapeutic aspects of masturbation was put forth by the Sufi scholar J.G. Bennett, who believed that talkativeness, greed, hyperactivity, inquisitiveness and even drug addiction are routinely used to discharge excess sexual energy. He wrote: 'For all those who are not committed to working on themselves for their transformation, masturbation acts like a safety valve for the sexual energy and allows it to be wasted without destructive consequences.'

However, masturbation can become a problem when it is utilized as a compulsive act or as a way to avoid entering into a relationship with another person. The hand can reveal why this situation exists, especially through examination of the lines of heart, head and union, in addition to the mount of Venus and the Mercury finger.

For example, a person with a low-level of self-esteem (as revealed by a short Jupiter finger and life and head lines that are joined), a sensitive, inward nature (as seen by a girdle of Venus, a long, chained 'mental' heart line, and a head and heart line that are close together) and problems with interpersonal communication (as shown by a low-set and short Mercury finger) may be likely to use chronic masturbation as a form of escape from relationship. This would be especially true if the mount of Venus is large, reddish and grilled, which indicates a strong sex drive and possible sexual excesses. Through the insights gained into the total personality picture, we can carefully advise how such a problem might be dealt with.

SAME-SEX ORIENTATION

The subject of homosexuality is a more serious issue, and nearly every book on palmistry has added to the confusion that exists regarding same-sex orientation. The hand of a homosexual – invariably a male – was portrayed as weak, with a supple thumb (revealing an unstable personality and a lack of will-power), a broken or islanded head line (indicating serious emotional problems) a long, broken girdle of Venus (betraying a sensitive nature and strong sexual appetites), a long, chained heart line (showing that emotions rule over reason) and pointy fingers (revealing artistic tendencies, capriciousness, and lack of emotional balance). I have not found this to be the case at all.

It is very difficult – if not impossible – to determine sexual orientation from the hand. People who prefer members of their own sex are found in every culture and profession, and represent a wide spectrum of personality traits and human emotions. According to D. J. West in his classic book *Homosexuality*,

> Some homosexuals suffer from neurotic fears and anxieties, and some are self-assured and hard as nails; some are vain and ostentatious and some are shy and quiet; some are cowardly and some are heroes; some are effeminate and some are brutes. Since all these types are represented, psychologists can too easily pick out examples to suit their pet theories.

Figure 8.1 is the print of a 43-year-old gay man. A former banker, he now works as a builder and lumberman while monitoring his Wall Street investments. His broad hands feature spatulate fingertips and a large mount of Venus, revealing a strong sensate nature, an open mind, a love of physical activity, and an ability to work well with three-dimensional reality. He also enjoys a reputation as an excellent masseur among both men and women. His abundant energy tends to be held in check, however, by the joining of the lines of life and

Figure 8.1: A gay man

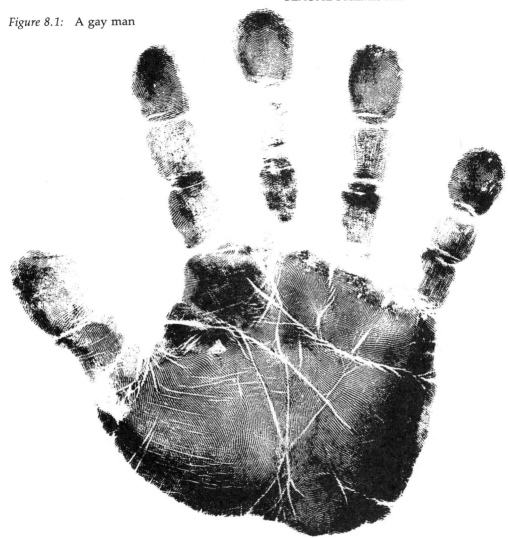

head, which indicate caution and introversion. The long, clear head line (especially as the subject enters into middle age) indicates a focused mind and strong intelligence. While the heart line is somewhat chained at its commencement, it does not indicate an inordinate amount of emotionality or sensitivity. Although the coarse appearance of the hand can be due in part to the type of work the subject performs, it is not the determining factor. His good ability to communicate (and business acumen) are found in his long Mercury finger. His 'line of adventure' (which moves horizontally across the mount of Luna, which we described in the previous chapter) is primarily reflected in his love of travel and working with nature and machinery.

Figure 8.2: A young man

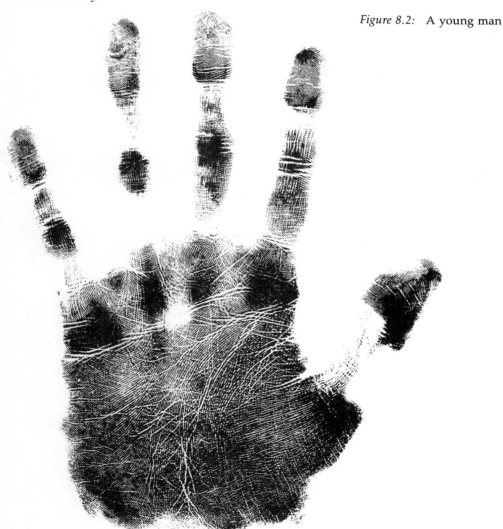

Figure 8.2 is the hand print of a young man whose hand closely resembles that of the stereotyped

homosexual described earlier: a long, broken heart line, a girdle of Venus, a flexible hand with a weak thumb, a weak and islanded head line, and numerous lines in general, which would indicate a tendency to be very emotional and highly strung.

The person in question does indeed manifest the psychological characteristics these aspects of the hand represent in real life, except that he prefers women over men, and has not felt the desire for a homosexual relationship.

Figure 8.3: A 28-year-old lesbian

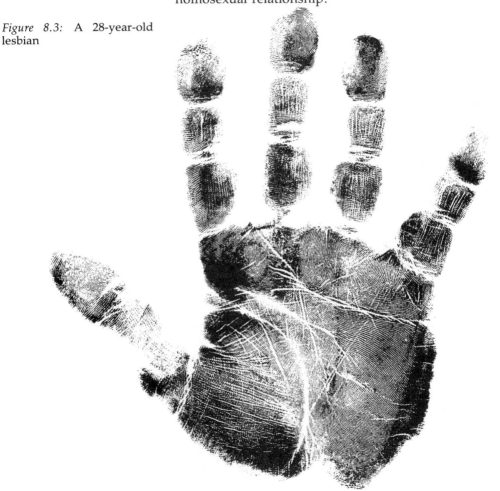

Figure 8.3 is the print of a 28-year-old lesbian, who works in hospital administration. Her squarish hand

reveals good organizational skills, and the deep head line (especially during her early and middle years) indicates mental clarity and focus. Although the subject comes across as 'tough' and 'butch' to strangers, she is actually very warm and caring, as shown by her long and sensitive heart line. Her innate impulsiveness and impatience is seen by the separation between the lines of head and life. In many aspects, her hand is no different to those of many heterosexually orientated women who are as dynamic and independent as she is.

These examples reveal that the boundaries between 'gay' and 'straight' are often quite vague, and blanket statements rarely serve a worthwhile purpose. The hand can, of course, provide important insights into the person's sensitivity, impressionability, emotional responsiveness, the degree of sexual repression operant in the personality, issues of aggressiveness and passivity, cruelty, the capacity to love and the ability to enjoy fulfilling relationships. Whether such feelings are directed primarily towards men or women (or both) is difficult to assess. Of course, if you know or intuitively feel that the person you are reading for is gay or bisexual, your consultation can be guided accordingly. For example, instead of speaking of the husband or wife they may have in the future, you can speak of a primary relationship without referring to gender.

SADISM AND MASOCHISM

Another often misunderstood form of sexual expression is sado-masochism or 'S and M'. Like the hand of a stereotyped homosexual, the 'sadist's hand', for example, has been portrayed by palmists as masculine, coarse and deep reddish in colour. The mounts of Venus and Mars are large and hard, and the fingers are often twisted. A 'murderer's thumb' is often featured as well. The problem is that there are people with such hands who are not sadistic, while some individuals with fine hands, long, slim fingers and fine skin texture can be very delicate about their cruelty, and act out their sadistic feelings every day of the week.

Sexually speaking, there are actually very few pure sadists or masochists, as most participants share both attributes. In essence, sexual sado-masochism is the ritual enactment of dominance and submission involving the use of pain, humiliation, trust/responsibility exchanges and controlled assaults to the body in order to achieve a high intensity of emotional and physical experience. For the most part, sado-masochism is a carefully monitored consensual activity, and considering its popularity in Western industrialized countries like the United States, Germany and the United Kingdom among men and women alike, serious injury or death is extremely rare.

People involve themselves in sado-masochism for a variety of reasons. Enthusiasts report that it gives them an emotional catharsis they would not normally experience in conventional sexual activity. Some are attracted to the dramatic and often theatrical aspects of role-playing in the sado-masochistic world, while others are drawn to the strong level of trust exchanged between partners during sado-masochistic activity. Others use it to expiate old guilts, to express feelings of cruelty, evil or violence, or to fully experience an intensely dominant or submissive role which they cannot otherwise experience in daily life. In *A Sexual Profile of Men in Power* the authors report a high frequency of sexual masochism (including verbal abuse and being tied up, beaten and humilated) among the political leaders and power brokers they studied. They concluded that the conflict between the two impulses of aggression and submission among these political and business leaders could lead to behaviour that swung widely between the opposite poles of ruthlessness (in the boardroom) and dependency (in the bedroom).

Some psychologists believe that people involved with sado-masochism have great difficulty getting in touch with their feelings. According to Dr Jack Lee Rosenberg in his book *Body, Self and Survival*, 'Whether they are thickly armored or split off, their inability to feel the subtle pleasures of sensuality leads them to seek greater stimulation by inflicting and receiving pain.'

As hand readers, we need to understand the

complexities of these issues, and try to comprehend the underlying reasons behind this type of sexual expression. Some participants may be seeking consciously or unconsciously to resolve major psychological issues in their lives, while others use sado-masochism to live 'on the periphery' and to avoid meaningful relationships of any kind.

For the most part, people involved with sado-masochism are not 'sick' and their hands may not be unlike those who indulge in more conventional sex. However, there are some features in the hand which

Figure 8.4: A bisexual woman involved in sado-masochism

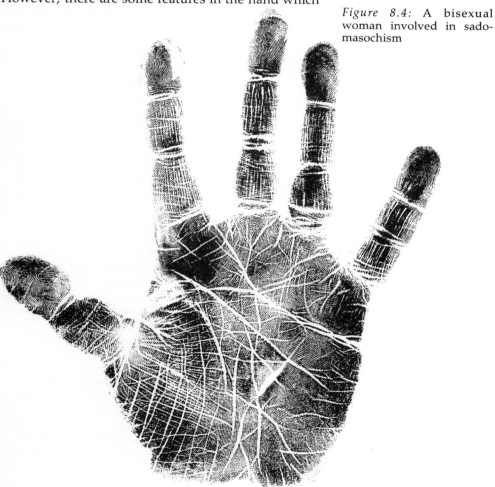

can indicate a desire for intense forms of sexual experience such as sado-masochism. They would include a strong, deep life line with a large mount of Venus, revealing an abundance of energy and stamina, especially if the thumb is strong and the hand is of firm consistency. A strong head line, a deep and possibly chained heart line, and a Simian line – would be indicative of an intense personality and strong character. Separated head and life lines would reveal a degree of sexual independence, as would a Mercury finger which stands apart from Apollo. If the person is fond of drama and role-playing, the Apollo finger would be long and well-formed. A person more interested in being the 'top' in sado-masochistic scenes would probably have a long Jupiter finger, a strong thumb and a large mount of lower Mars, especially if this role involves an active physical dynamic like whipping.

While many of these traits are found in the hand of the 24-year-old bisexual woman who is involved in sado-masochistic sex (figure 8.4) we cannot conclude that all devotees of sado-masochism will have similar hand characteristics. As with gays, vegetarians or born-again Christians, people involved in sado-masochism belong to all kinds of professions and political persuasions, and represent nearly every personality type known in psychology.

Like sexual preference, the boundaries between having sado-masochistic inclinations and acting them out is often very fine. Psychologists tell us that nearly everyone has entertained thoughts of sexual sadism or masochism at one time or another, even though such feelings are seldom, if ever expressed.

OTHER VARIATIONS

Other avenues of sexual expression include voyeurism, fetishism, exhibitionism and cross-dressing. Long viewed as serious acts of perversion by society, such activities are today seen as relatively benign, especially if they do not involve the forced participation of children or unwilling adults. Very often, these activities are expressions of energetic blocks on both physical and psychological levels, and may have their roots in loneliness, sexual repression, fear, or lack of self-esteem. Like other sexual practices, they should be of concern to the hand reader if they cause the subject to avoid deep relationships with others and bring about depression as the result of guilt or fear.

As mentioned before, many people have experienced the desire to be a voyeur or to dress in clothes normally worn by members of the opposite sex. Whether one actually partakes of such activities has not only to do with one's level of interest, but

Figure 8.5: A cross-dresser

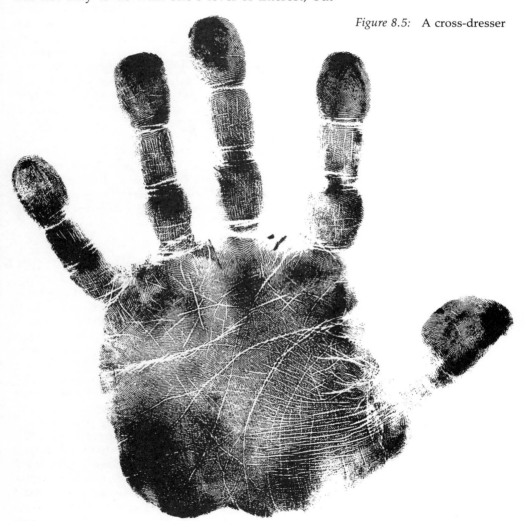

also with the shedding of previous conditioning against such taboos. Figure 8.5, for example, is the hand print of a 30-year-old male accountant who frequently dresses in women's clothing. The fact that he works for a large Fifth Avenue department store enables him to purchase many of his dresses, shoes, cosmetics and wigs at a special employee's discount. The palm itself does not offer any specific clues which would reveal that the subject enjoys cross-dressing. However, the strong Apollo finger and accompanying line of Apollo would indicate a love of beauty and flair for style, which could be reflected in art, music or the way one dresses. The long (and independent) Mercury finger would reveal both a nonconformist's way of seeing the world, as well as an ability to communicate with others. The sloping head line would reveal a strong imagination, although it is balanced by an upwardly moving branch, adding an accountant's practicality. In general, the person is cautious, careful and somewhat secretive (as seen by the joining of the lines of life and head and the narrow space between the heart and head lines). I read the subject's hand during a flight to Rio de Janeiro, where he was making a pilgrimage to the Carmen Miranda Museum.

SEXUAL ABUSE OF CHILDREN

Child abuse is a far more serious matter, although it is still little understood. As both a social and sexual issue, child abuse (which often involves incest) is rarely dealt with by society, despite its widespread and frequent occurrence. In many cases, the stigma is placed on the young victim rather than on the perpetrator, who is often a relative or trusted adult.

Before we proceed, it is important to distinguish between child abuse (which involves an older person imposing himself or herself sexually on a young child) and consensual intergenerational sex, where a young person (usually a teenager) chooses to engage in sexual activity with an older person over the legal age of consent. Although laws in a country like the United States prohibit sex between adults and people under the age of 16 or 18 (as the case may be) the fact is that many teenagers are both physically and psychologically mature enough to choose their sexual partners without being coerced by an adult.

A major characteristic among child abusers is that they themselves were abused as children. In the hand, this may be seen as a major influence line crossing both the life and head lines. In some instances, it may even cross the heart line as well.

People who abuse children sexually are emotionally disturbed. In many instances, this can be seen by an islanded head line, as well as a 'string of pearls' dermoglyphic pattern, an indicator of neurosis. Where sexual drive is strong, a large, reddish mount of Venus would be present. A tendency towards violence would be seen by large, coarse mounts of Mars, reddish nails and a coarse skin texture.

One would assume that people who impose themselves sexually on children would have no control over their sexual proclivities (hence, a supple thumb or flexible hand) but studies reveal that child abusers can be wilful and stubborn. Many are often unable or unwilling to respond to psychological treatment.

Like other forms of sexual practice we have examined in this chapter, it is extremely difficult to look at someone's hand and say 'This person is a child molester'. For this reason, we need to carefully examine the hand as a total unit and be open to intuitive perceptions regarding the total psychosexual picture.

However, there are a number of important features in the hand which may be indicative of serious sexual problems which not only involve abnormal behaviour, but the potential of violence towards others. Such markings can reveal a tendency to go beyond the normal boundaries of adventurous sex and into realms of sexual conduct that pose a danger to others.

Signs of severe psychosexual problems include the following:

1. Hands and fingers which are abnormally short or long when compared to the individual's body size.
2. The Jupiter and Saturn fingers being of equal length, or the Saturn and Apollo fingers being of equal length. Dr Charlotte Wolfe, author of *The*

Hand in Psychological Diagnosis found that such configurations appear primarily among schizophrenics.

3. Fingers that are severely twisted or deformed (especially the fingers of Jupiter and Mercury) when not the result of arthritis or injury.
4. Severely chained, broken and islanded head lines.
5. Head lines that are missing (especially in both hands) or extremely weak or short head lines (particularly when accompanied by a strong, deep heart line and large, reddish and coarsely textured mount of Venus).
6. A thumb that is abnormally short, deformed, or placed extremely high on the hand to the extent that it appears similar to that of an infant.
7. An abnormally large, hard and red mount of Venus, especially if the skin is coarse and grilled.
8. Abnormally large and red mounts of Upper and Lower Mars, especially when present with the type of Venus mount described above.
9. A Simian line found on a rough and poorly shaped hand, particularly when the hand features two or more of the characteristics listed above.

It should be remembered that the existence of one or two of these traits does not mean that the individual is a sexual psychopath or rapist. As mentioned before, the features of the hand reveal *potential*. In addition, modifying factors in the hand have been known to counteract negative qualities found in hand shape, fingers and lines.

DESIRE DISORDERS: IMPOTENCE AND FRIGIDITY

On the other end of the scale, there are people with problems of sexual functioning. There are physical, energetic and psychological causes for so-called 'desire disorders' which include blocked sexual desire, inhibited sexual excitement, the inability to achieve orgasm, inhibition of arousal, premature ejaculation, or outright aversion to sex.

While there are no clear-cut indications of these

sexual problems in the hand, one can observe several markings on the palm which may contribute to the problem. A small, weak or very soft mount of Venus and a thin hand of flabby consistency would indicate a low level of sexual vitality. A life line cutting through a normal-sized mount of Venus would tend to cancel out much of the warmth and passion this mount would normally provide. A weak heart line would indicate that sexual expression is not a major priority in life. An influence line joining or breaking the heart line may reveal a major emotional trauma that would affect the person's sexual desire. Finally, indicators of physical illness* (as seen on the life line as well as related lines of heart, head and stomach) may have a bearing on sexual interest and the ability to function in a sexual way.

Sometimes people 'turn off' sexually as a defence from feeling. Individuals with a long, chained and deep heart line – especially if it drops down to join both the lines of head and life – can be afraid of their feelings to such a degree that they simply 'split off' on both emotional and sexual levels. While they may appear cold and aloof to their partner, the reality is that they are scared of their feelings, whether they involve dependency, yearning or anger. In addition, these emotional expressions are often connected with energetic blocks in the body, which impede the free flowing of energy during the sexual act. The reader is invited to consult Alexander Lowen's book *Love and Orgasm* (see bibliography) for further discussion.

However, other factors should be considered. While the hand characteristics mentioned above may reveal potential, the actual relationship between the two people involved is of primary importance. Before we consider an individual problem, we should view it in the light of *that specific relationship* and the conscious or unconscious energetic connection between the partners. In that relationship, the woman may be frigid or the man may be impotent. Different people react in different ways depending on their 'chemistry' together, negative past experiences, anger, jealousy or issues of guilt or sexual repression. Stress in their job or other external factors may also

*For further discussion, consult chapter 9 of *The Palmistry Workbook* (Aquarian Press, 1984).

be involved. Remember to observe the problem in the context of the relationship (which will be explored further in the following chapter). However, if the problem is chronic – meaning that the man has been unable to function sexually in his four previous relationships as well – it is more an individual problem and should be dealt with accordingly.

Remember that people who are anxious, repressed or angry are not necessarily impotent or frigid, so general statements should be avoided. However, if sexual dysfunction is mentioned by the person as a problem, a hand analyst can offer many useful insights regarding the primary issues that can prevent this individual from enjoying a fulfilling sexual relationship with another.

When we have the opportunity to counsel others through hand analysis, we have a responsibility to help them get in touch with their reality. At the same time, we must strengthen this self-awareness with inspiration and constructive advice to help them take the next step. By learning how to contact the deepest essence of those who seek our help regarding sexual expression or sexual problems, we can serve as an effective catalyst for helping them realize their true potential for personal growth and happiness.

Chapter 9

COMPATIBILITY IN RELATIONSHIPS

There are many reasons why people choose to become romantically involved. On one level, some individuals are lonely and simply want steady company. Others feel that a partner will provide a psychological trait or characteristic they may lack within themselves. Still others pursue a relationship to achieve respectability, status, or to enjoy regular sex. There are other, more important reasons as well. For some, their attraction to another person may produce a primal 'chemistry' on physical, emotional and even spiritual levels. Whether their personalities are similar or opposite, the attraction is profound, and they want to explore and deepen their connection. For others, relationship can be a primary avenue for personal growth and spiritual evolution. According to John L. Hoff in his essay 'Practical Friendship'

> We need to know how to build relationship and how to use that field of force as an energy to nurture and guide us – it is our primary resource for human evolution and spiritual development. It is in relationships that we collaborate with each other to create a better world.

Whether we wish to study our own hands, or choose to read the hands of others, it is important that we have a basic understanding of the dynamics of human relationship and how a relationship can affect one's life. Being deeply involved with another person (whether this develops into an actual marriage or not) often brings up important emotional material we can often avoid dealing with when we are alone. Our ability to trust, to make compromises, to be vulnerable or to share feelings is constantly challenged in a close relationship. When we are romantically involved with another person, we are called upon to accept our partner totally, despite his or her imperfections. As we learn to accept our partner, we come closer to accepting other people as well. On both psychological and spiritual levels, we become more at one with the world.

Many people are in deep confusion about marriage and committed relationships. All too often, society sets marriage up as the ideal for every person and has provided tax benefits and other advantages for those whose unions are sanctioned by the government or church. According to popular belief, a marriage should be both exclusive and last for ever. Unfortunately, the sad reality of a 30–50 per cent divorce rate among couples living in industrialized Western countries – with its accompanying emotional, financial and social trauma – points out the difficulties of this marriage ideal.

When we examine potential relationships in another's hand we should be aware of the possibility that marriage (or even a committed relationship) may not be advisable. Many people are not ready for marriage and should not be coerced into it. For some, the freedom of being single, with its inherent versatility, independence and freedom from compromise, may be more important at that point in their lives than a marriage or exclusive partnership.

However, those who are contemplating an important relationship need to understand their true motivations, in addition to becoming aware of any fears or psychological blocks which can prevent them from achieving a relationship that is pleasurable and which offers an opportunity for deep contact and personal growth. Those who are already in a relationship need to be made aware of the potential strengths and weaknesses in their union so that they can reach greater levels of harmony and intimacy with their partners. A major task of a hand analyst is to help others achieve greater self-awareness and self-knowledge so that their present or future relationship can be determined less by the expectations of society and more by their own genuine needs and aspirations. In the following pages we will explore how the hand can help us reach this important goal of self-understanding and unfoldment.

LINES OF UNION

The so-called 'marriage lines' in the hand are actually lines of union. They indicate the potential of an important relationship in a person's life and the possible age at which it will occur. Lines of union are located between the heart line and the Mercury finger, and move horizontally from the percussion edge of the hand across the mount of Mercury. The earlier the relationship occurs, the lower on the hand it appears, while subsequent relationships will appear higher on the mount, as seen in figure 9.1. However, it should be noted that in countries where early marriages are common (in India, for example, many people marry at fifteen or sixteen years of age) we would need to revise our estimate accordingly. The length of the line not only indicates the potential life of the relationship, but its importance in the person's life as well.

Figure 9.1: Union lines

As we mentioned before, the union line can indicate the potential of an important relationship with a man or a woman, which may or may not be sexual in nature. In some cases – as in the hands of people whose legal marriage is superficial or psychologically distant – a strong line of union can indicate a close friend with whom there is a primary (though not necessarily sexual) relationship. For the most part, this 'union' is not with a close relative like a parent, sibling or child, but with someone not of the family. The hand print segment in figure 9.2 reveals two major lines of union. The early, primary union was a thirty year marriage, which ended with the death of the husband. The second line represents a best friend; a close non-sexual relationship which has

119

endured for nearly forty years.

For this reason, it is sometimes difficult to judge whether a line of union indicates a traditional marriage or not. Because hand analysis is an art as well as a science, the reader's intuition can play a role in evaluating both the present and future existence of a marriage-type relationship.

Ideally, the union line should be clear, straight and long, and free of islands and breaks. The longer and deeper the line, the longer and more important the relationship. Islands and breaks on a union line reveal a corresponding weakness in the relationship at the approximate age shown on the line. Unfortunately there is no certain sign of age on a union line, as its length can also reveal the lingering impact of a relationship on the person even after it is 'officially' over. Again, the intuition can be useful here. Major issues involving incompatibility,

Figure 9.2: Union lines

Figure 9.3: Change in union lines (a)

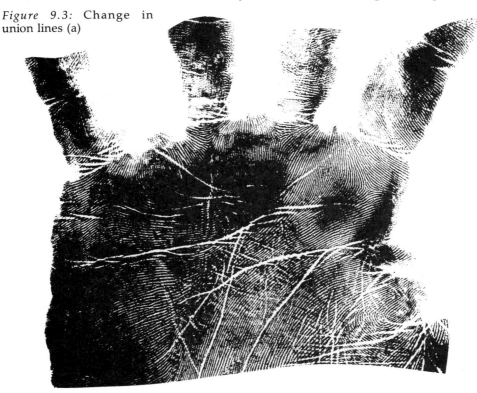

personality conflicts, lack of commitment and infidelity are often reflected in islands or breaks.

Whenever you study a union line, remember that it is subject to change. Figure 9.3 for example, was taken when the subject was 23 years old. He had no real interest in marriage and doubted that it would

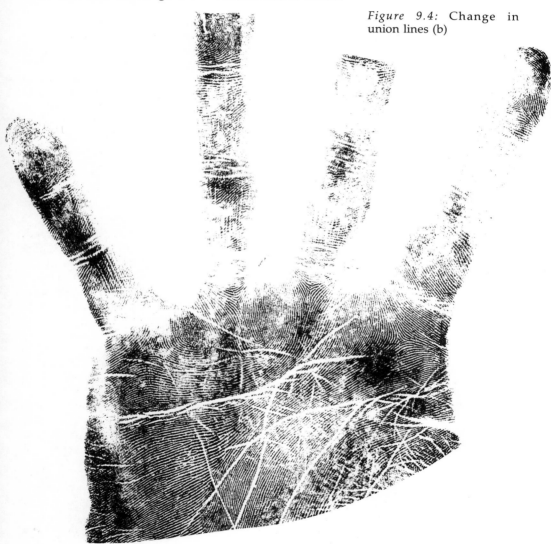

Figure 9.4: Change in union lines (b)

ever happen. The line itself is weak and broken, revealing the potential for a difficult relationship which would probably not endure. Several years later, he met a woman and fell in love. After they married, his union line began to change, as seen in figure 9.4. The fragmented line grew deeper and longer. The marriage is loving and harmonious, with a potential to continue for many happy years.

For this reason, readers should be careful about making predictions like 'you will divorce by the time you are forty' or 'you will never get married'. In addition to the probability of being incorrect, you may also be creating self-fulfilling prophesies in the person's life. If you see a possible separation, for example, it is much more helpful to state 'I see a possible break-up unless you and your husband work on this relationship.' You not only point out a potential problem, but also help the person to take control of the situation rather than leave it to 'fate'.

From my experience, a union line which droops downwards towards its conclusion indicates that the subject's partner will probably die first. When it is split, a break-up of the relationship may be indicated, or the union will go through a major transition which can change both the tenor and the direction of the relationship entirely. This often occurs at the so-called 'midlife crisis' when the children leave home and thus cease to be a major focus in the couple's life.

According to Andrew Fitzherbert, a fork at the end of a union line can reveal a messy divorce. Rather than concluding the relationship by mutual agreement, he feels that such a line would indicate a termination filled with pain, trauma and recrimination.

In rare cases, the union line either droops downwards or upwards radically, as shown in figure 9.5. When this occurs, it reveals that it is difficult for the person to establish any deep attachment, and it is unlikely that a marriage-quality relationship can ever take place. An absence of a union line would point to a similar state of affairs, while tiny, weak union lines would reveal short and possibly superficial relationships which would not last for more than several years each.

Figure 9.5: A drooping union line

DETERMINING COMPATIBILITY

One of the more exciting trends in modern palmistry is a compatibility study of the hands of both partners to determine areas of potential harmony and conflict, as well as issues of jealousy, withdrawal and domination discussed earlier in this book. Offering information regarding a couple's compatibility requires great care on the part of the hand reader, and should only be attempted after the palmist has gained much experience in hand analysis.

There are, of course, many reasons (both obvious and hidden) why two people decide to form a marriage or love relationship. They may share common interests and enjoy each other's company. They may have good sexual rapport, but like to pursue their own personal goals. Some people thrive on being with someone radically different to themselves, and many couples remain close through friction and even conflict. Some are together because they like their partner's appearance, wit or bank account. Others may be spiritually compatible, or move in the same political or social circles. In some cases, the relationship may be bound by ancient 'karmic ties' and the couple are together because they need to resolve old issues between them from a past life. Such relationships can often be quite difficult, but are extremely important for the parties concerned. For these reasons, the hand reader must be extremely careful when making pronouncements on the advisability of establishing or continuing a relationship. While the palmist can provide a highly valuable service by making both people aware of the inherent strengths and weaknesses of their relationship through a careful and thorough analysis of their hands, one must leave any decisions about the future of the relationship itself to the people involved.

While marriage counsellors do not have a perfect formula to guarantee a strong, lasting and harmonious union, experts have recognized several important factors which can contribute to a relationship that will grow deeper and stronger over the years.

Perhaps the primary consideration has to do with similarities and differences between the two people involved. In *The Psychology of Sex*, the authors point out that 'partnerships are more successful if based on similarities rather than supposed complementation' and that marriage bureaux agree that similar personality traits and interests are crucial to successful long-term relationships. On the other hand, some point out that there is often more opportunity for growth in a relationship of opposites, as each partner can learn more about themselves and their relationship through the friction generated by being with someone who is very dissimilar.

When we consider these polarities, perhaps the ideal relationship would be with someone with whom there are similarities in areas of real importance, while allowing room for enough differences to help make the relationship more interesting. Ideally, each person would share (or at least respect) the partner's views on major issues like religion, politics and the desire to have children. They would also hopefully share basic views on matters like diet, smoking and sex.

Aside from sexual attraction, the couple should be sexually compatible both energetically and psychologically. If the relationship has a good sexual foundation, it has a greater potential for long-term success. Closely connected to sex is the ability to communicate. In addition to aiding in the practical resolution of conflicts inherent in any relationship, good communication enables two people to know each other deeply. They are able to achieve a relationship based on mutual trust and appreciation. Through open and positive communication, each person can learn to reinforce the partner's strengths rather than just compensating for weaknesses.

However, the key to a successful relationship would involve compatibility on several levels (i.e. physical, emotional, mental and spiritual) rather than on sexual compatibility or mental stimulation alone. According to Omraam Mikhaël Aivenov in his book *Love and Sexuality.*

The ideal is to agree on all three planes, to have a mutual physical attraction, a similarity of tastes and feelings ... and most important of all, there must be a tremendous agreement in the world of ideas, a common goal, an ideal.

COMPATIBILITY: WHAT YOUR HANDS REVEAL

When undertaking a compatibility study for a couple, there are several aspects of the hand which require special attention. While differences in one or two areas would not necessarily be cause for concern, several areas of major difference could indicate a difficult relationship in which the potential for compatibility would be poor.

Because the *shape* of the hand reveals basic temperament, it should lay the foundation for a compatibility analysis. If one partner has squarish hands while the other partner's hands are conic, the couple will probably have a very different way of seeing the world. While the owner of the squarish hand would tend to be highly organized, practical and enjoy rules and structure in relationship, his partner would tend towards the instinctual, spontaneous and romantic. Be sure to examine both hands thoroughly to find either confirming or modifying aspects. For example, a squarish hand with a separation between the lines of life and head would increase spontaneity, while a conic hand with a long, straight head line would increase the tendency to be practical and realistic. Similarities in hand and thumb flexibility and in hand consistency should also be roughly compatible, thus assuring a degree of harmony in the way the couple face the challenges of life and adapt to the world around them.

Because the mount of Venus is our primary indicator of physical and sexual energy, it is vitally important as a factor in analysing compatibility. Ideally, both people should have mounts of Venus of comparable size to their respective physical builds. If one person has a strong sex drive while the other does not, serious problems may result which can sabotage an otherwise harmonious relationship.

Closely related to sexual energy is sexual personality, which is largely determined by the heart line. If both people share a deep 'physical' heart line, they both enjoy the purely sexual aspects of love, while people with straight 'mental' heart lines place more importance on soft music, cuddling and emotional support. While variations are inevitable, a person with a short physical heart line ending under the mount of Saturn and another with a long, mental heart line ending under Jupiter would probably be very incompatible on sexual levels. Whether or not having different types and sizes of heart lines will present a problem in a relationship can be determined by studying other aspects of the hand, including the mount of Venus (revealing sex drive), the Mercury finger (showing the ability to communicate with one's partner) and hand motility, which could reveal one's ability to adapt to another person's sexual style.

Another related issue of compatibility would be sensitivity. Ideally, the degree of sensitivity between two people in a relationship should be approximately the same, so that there is a greater potential to be aware of the partner's feelings and needs. While fine skin or lots of lines are clear indications of a sensitive nature, a chained or fretted heart line is also important, because it reflects deep emotions as well. However, if both people appear to be overly sensitive (as shown by the hand print in figure 9.6) their relationship could be somewhat difficult, as both parties could overreact to almost any conflict or problem and blow it completely out of proportion. If one person is slightly less sensitive than the other, there is a greater chance for counterpoint and balance.

Stiff thumbs and rigid hands indicate a tendency to be strong-willed and stubborn. When both people share this trait, neither would want to compromise over an issue or a problem. For this reason, it is important that we examine other aspects of the hands to determine whether the couple is at least compatible in major areas, so that their inherent stubbornness will be confined to minor issues. In such cases, a hand reader might offer the suggestion that each person become aware of their wilfulness and strive to develop the qualities of compromise and understanding for the other person's point of view.

Other factors, such as intelligence, emotional stability, reliability, self-esteem, patience, impulsiveness, temper and the ability to communicate, may play a major role in helping determine a compatible relationship. For this reason, the palmist should have a thorough grounding in the science of hand analysis in order to achieve an accurate overview of all aspects

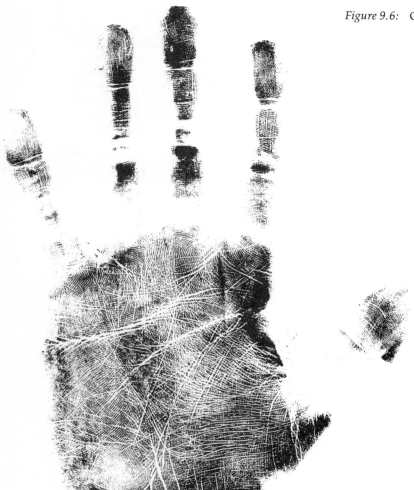

Figure 9.6: Over-sensitivity

of the hand both individually and as part of a total psychological picture.

Whenever we counsel an individual or couple, the best service we can provide is to enable them to become more aware of *who they are* and help them achieve a deeper understanding of their individual strengths and weaknesses and how these can manifest as potential barriers and hidden potentials in their relationship. By clarifying the issues and

127

helping each person become aware of his psycho-sexual nature and how it can affect the relationship, we help them take personal responsibility for their life.

However, unless we are trained in marriage counselling or psychotherapy, we should avoid specific counselling or therapy of any kind. Sharing information and good advice is one thing, and practising therapy is another. Whenever we feel that such services are needed by the person we are reading for, we should refer him or her to the appropriate professional.

SECTION III:
PRACTICE

By this time you should have a thorough conceptual grounding in the essence of psychosexual hand analysis. In the following chapters we will examine the more practical 'how-to' aspects of reading hands and taking hand prints.

Chapter 10
HOW TO READ HANDS

Reading the hand of another person is a very serious matter, involving tremendous responsibility. Simply stated, hand analysis involves one person letting another person study a part of his or her body and then make pronouncements on highly personal and sensitive issues, such as sexuality. In a sense, hand analysis can be compared to reading someone's private letters or journals. For this reason, a hand reader must bear responsibility for both what is said and how it is expressed during a consultation.

The underlying intent of the hand reader is of primary importance. Hand analysis must never be used to impress or seduce, or to gain power or control over another's life. Efforts must be made to be as objective as possible, while maintaining close contact with the other person during the reading. Honesty is an essential component of each hand analysis, yet we must phrase every observation and suggestion in a way that is truthful, kind and non-judgemental. If what we have to say does not satisfy these three requirements, it is better to say nothing.

At the same time, we need to avoid the tendency to focus only on the positive aspects of the hand. While we should help the individual become aware of his talents and abilities, we do him no favour by glossing over negative aspects or areas of conflict in his life, especially when they relate to matters of sexuality and relationship.

Closely related to this issue is *timing*. In certain situations it is not appropriate to reveal information, especially if we feel that it would cause unnecessary pain or if the person would not be able to deal with the particular issue or problem.

Although our primary goal should be to help those who come to us for a consultation, it is important to realize that, as hand readers, we are not practising therapy, especially sex therapy. Therapy involves a regular, ongoing process in the deep psychological change of the individual which should only be performed by a qualified psychologist or sex therapist.

Counselling, on the other hand, is relatively brief and is usually intended to work with specific areas of concern, such as health, career or relationship. Although a hand reader's task often involves some degree of counselling, it is not our major goal. Rather, our primary task is that of *education,* involving a one-time consultation consisting of the simple sharing of information. The person receiving the reading wants to be told about him or herself with the goal of expanding self-knowledge and personal well-being. While it is possible that a consultation may lead the individual to seek counselling or therapy, this is not the reader's main task. For this reason, many chirologists discourage frequent consultations (usually limiting them to one or two a year) while referring the 'client' to an appropriate counsellor or therapist as needed.

Perhaps one of the most difficult lessons for the hand reader is to take a personal interest in the client while remembering that the client is responsible for his or her life. Nevertheless, when major life issues are exposed and discussed, we should never leave the client hanging, but should try to lead him or her to the 'next step' whenever possible. According to Stephen Arroyo in his excellent book *Astrology, Psychology and the Four Elements:*

One should realize that merely giving advice without also giving a means for deeper understanding is of little value, for each person must do his or her own work and must, through his or her own experience, arrive at the higher awareness that enables the person to outgrow or transcend the difficulty.

In addition to possible referral to a counsellor or therapist, such a process may involve eliciting reactions and questions, so that the client will take a more active role in the reading rather than being merely a passive listener. This participation also leads to their seeking solutions to problems by themselves. Very often we know the solutions to our problems on a deep level, but are accustomed to avoiding them or having someone else provide the solution.

Respect for privacy is often overlooked by hand readers. In my own work, I prefer to read an individual's hands alone, in a quiet setting, without the involvement of a third party looking on, making comments or asking questions. In the case of compatibility readings for a couple, it may be preferable to read each person's hands first without the other partner present, and then join the two of them for a discussion of their hands.

Although a tape recorder sometimes encourages the client to pay less attention to the reading as it is being given, I do not object to its use. I never discuss a reading with others; at the time I read someone's hand it is *our* business, but after the consultation is over, the information discussed is no longer my affair. This is especially important to remember when we are discussing matters of sex.

There is no one method or technique to reading a hand. Although I encourage each reader to develop a method which works best for him or her, the following general procedure may be helpful.

PREPARATION

Before you are to read another's hand, try to become aware of both the privilege and the responsibility involved. Meditation and prayer are useful to help you get grounded in your 'core' or higher self, and to come into closer contact with your intuition.

Before you look at the person's hands, ask if he or she has ever had a reading before. Point out that the hands show tendencies and not always definite facts, and that the lines on the hand can change within a matter of weeks. Ask the person's age and find out if they are right- or left-handed. Explain that the passive hand is more the storehouse of our potential while the active hand more clearly expresses what we are doing with it.

LOOKING AT THE HANDS

Sitting directly across from the client, take both hands in yours and look at them. Close your eyes for a moment and say a silent prayer to help you focus and do your best. I prefer a simple 'Thy will be done' while a friend prefers 'I pray that all I may now tell him/her will be for his/her highest good and for the highest good of all concerned.' This momentary spiritual focusing need not be so obvious as to be noticed by the person you are reading for, but can appear as though you are merely collecting your thoughts before proceeding with the reading.

Look carefully at both hands. Take note of the size, shape, skin texture and flexibility. Note the positions and lengths of the fingers, taking account of the basic hand types. Don't be afraid to touch, bend and squeeze the hand gently as you examine it.

Observe the fingers carefully, taking special note of their size, flexibility, shape and contour. Are any of the fingers bent? Which are prominent and which are weak? How are they held on the hand?

Turn the hands over and observe the nails, and ask the person to open the hands wide. Check out the knots of the fingers as well as the relative position of the fingers to each other and to the hand as a whole.

Turn the hands over again and examine the mounts. Run your finger over each of the mounts and judge their relative strengths. Note any special markings on the mounts, such as squares, crosses and grilles.

Look at the lines, taking careful notice of their strength, clarity and length. Where do they begin and where do they end? Are there breaks, dots or islands on the lines? Are there branches or colour changes? How do the lines differ on each hand?

After examining the hands for a few minutes, you

will get a 'feel' for the hand and a basic understanding of who the person is you are reading for. At
this point, take the active hand and begin reading,
being ready to look at the passive hand for
confirming or contrasting traits. Begin the reading at
a point which feels most appropriate. With some
people you may want to begin with a general
character analysis, while with others, you might
begin directly with matters of sexuality and
relationship. Use your judgement.

Proceed slowly through your reading, always
being open to intuitive messages from your
subconscious. Make frequent eye contact with the
client. You may prefer to answer questions during
the reading, or ask for questions when you are done.

Throughout the reading, try to keep the following
issues in the back of your mind and ask yourself if
you are dealing with them.

1. What is the person really looking for?
2. What is he/she ready to hear?
3. Is what I am saying appropriate for the person at
    this time?
4. What is the best way to help this person develop
    his/her sense of initiative, responsibility and
    participation in life?
5. Does this reading touch on sensitive issues of my
    own which may affect the reading and my
    objectivity? (This is especially important in
    dealing with matters of sexuality.)
6. Am I making myself clear and am I being
    understood?

When practised with care, sensitivity and
humility, hand analysis can be an endless source of
adventure, learning and inspiration. By helping
others increase their self-knowledge and self-
acceptance, we invariably increase our own. By
helping others 'remove the stones from the path' we
open our own channel of compassion and service.

Chapter 11

HOW TO TAKE HAND PRINTS

Figure 11.1: Rolling out the ink

Figure 11.2: Inking the hand

One of the best ways to deepen our understanding of the hand is to maintain a record of the hands we analyse. Although plaster casts of hands faithfully show the form and lines, they are complicated to make and difficult to store. Photographs of the hands are simpler to make and easier to store, but often involve considerable expense.

The easiest and cheapest method of recording hands is the taking of palm prints. Although the prints do not always reveal the exact hand shape, lines and ridges can be – with practice – faithfully reproduced. When used with the Hand Analysis Test Chart described later on, a collection of hand prints can be very useful. In addition to providing a permanent record of the hand itself, subsequent follow-up prints can reveal changes in the hand over the years.

Materials

The materials necessary for taking hand prints are both inexpensive and easy to obtain:

1. A rubber roller approximately four inches (10 cm) wide.

2. A tube of black water-base block printing (lino) ink.
3. Good quality art paper. You may prefer single sheets, or a spiral-bound art book for easier storage.
4. A thin pad of foam rubber to provide a suitable cushion for the paper.
5. A sheet of glass, linoleum or newspaper for applying the ink.

Procedure

Figure 11.3: Placing the hand on the paper

1. First, you lay the paper over the foam rubber, which helps mould the paper to conform to the contours of the hand. Roll out the ink on the glass, linoleum or newspaper (figure 11.1).
2. Carefully ink the subject's hand, using just enough ink to lightly cover the entire palmar surface (figure 11.2).
3. Have the subject place their hand on the paper in a natural way. Apply pressure to the entire hand (paying special attention to the centre of the palm and the space between the finger mounts) in order to obtain a complete impression (figure 11.3).
4. Hold the paper to the table as the hand is slowly withdrawn. This will prevent the print from blurring (figure 11.4).

Figure 11.4: Holding the paper to prevent blurring

In addition to the print itself, you should include a record of the major features of the hand, such as the shape, dominant fingers and mounts, as well as personal data concerning the individual whose print you are including in your collection. A suggested Hand Analysis Test Chart follows for your convenience.

HAND ANALYSIS TEST CHART

Name:
Date of birth:
Today's date:

Predominant hand type
Strongest mounts
Weakest mounts

Tests
Skin texture
Skin colour
Flexibility
Consistency

Fingers (describe)
Jupiter
Saturn
Apollo
Mercury
Predominant
Longer or shorter than palm
Straight
Bent

Thumb
Size
Flexibility
How set (low, medium, high)
Will phalange (describe)
Logic phalange (describe)

Nails
Size
Shape
Colour
Unusual features

Additional comments/personal data

Chapter 12

ANALYSIS OF HAND PRINTS

On the following pages, we will analyse the hands of several couples and individuals from the author's collection of prints.

ANALYSIS 1 (Figures 12.1 and 12.2)

The prints reproduced here are of a couple who recently celebrated their fortieth wedding anniversary. While each person is different to the other both in character and professional interest (the wife is an artist while the husband is a mathematician), they find that their life together offers both strong similarities and contrasts.

Their joined head and life lines indicate a shared caution and a tendency to depend on the other. Both are intelligent (as seen by their head lines), have comparable sized mounts of Venus, somewhat similar heart lines, and share an ability to communicate well with the other. They also share a love for art, music and motoring.

While they are in basic agreement on most important issues, they have different ways of seeing the world. The husband tends to be more conservative and rational, while the wife is more rebellious, and eager to explore new ideas and trends. In addition, she tends to be more restless and emotional, as seen by the numerous lines in her hand and her sensitive heart line. Although both enjoy being together, each partner gives the other lots of physical and psychological space to pursue his or her separate interests. Each has more than one union line, which reveals other deep friendships in addition to their marriage.

Figure 12.1: Analysis 1 (a)

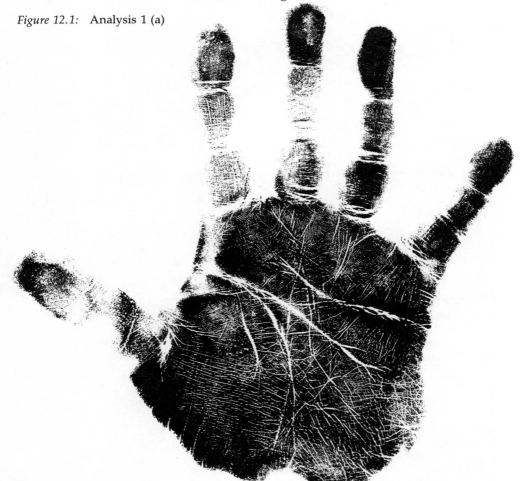

When problems arise in the relationship, they make an effort to seek compromise, as both have stiff

Figure 12.2: Analysis 1 (b)

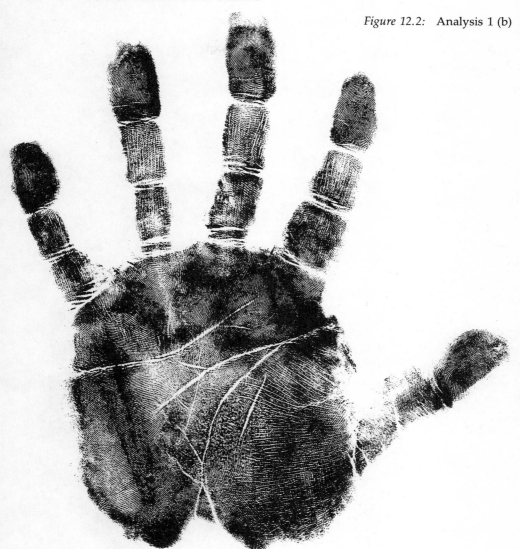

thumbs and relatively inflexible hands. As the hands are somewhat similiar in shape, they are both fairly rational and practical in the way they deal with challenges and new situations.

The essence of their relationship involves a balance between both interdependence and dependence, with a strong sense of shared affection, loyalty and mutual respect.

141

ANALYSIS 2 (Figures 12.3 and 12.4)

Figure 12.3: Analysis 2 – Richard

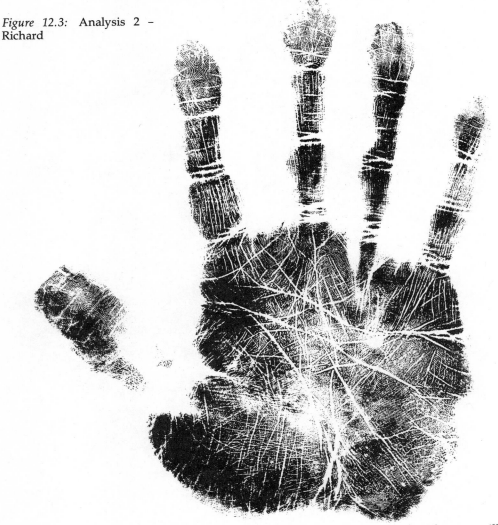

These prints are those of a gay couple who we will call Richard and Dale. They first met in the army twenty-nine years ago, when Richard was a colonel and Dale was a corporal. They fell in love and have been together ever since, both as partners in a monogamous relationship and as co-owners of a successful business.

Figure 12.4: Analysis 2 –
Dale

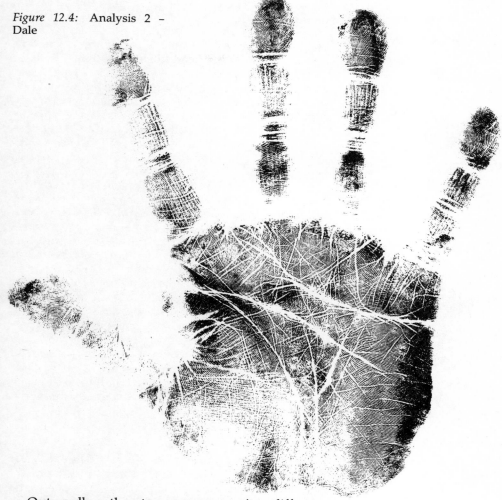

Outwardly, the two appear quite different.
Richard, who is 74, is more the 'colonel' and is seen
as more mature, more decisive and the stronger of
the two. Dale, who is 52, is viewed as more the
'corporal' and is more relaxed, carefree and
compliant.

However an examination of their hands reveals
strong personalities for each partner, with many
areas of similarity. The hand shapes are similar,
although the fingers on Dale's hand are shorter when

compared to the size of his palm, revealing a strong instinctual nature. Richard's fingers are comparably longer, and his knotted fingers show his tendency to analyse and focus on details. Both men are very intelligent, and their head lines are roughly equal in length and move in the same direction. Their heart lines are similar as well, except that Dale's is slightly more 'physical' and reveals a bit more sensitivity than Richard's. The mounts of Venus are approximately the same size, both hands feature 'samaritan lines', and their Saturn lines reveal successful careers. Both Richard and Dale are good communicators, and enjoy talking with each other.

Both men have firm hands and strong 'stubborn' thumbs (especially Dale), revealing that he has his way more than others might think. However, both men agree on most issues, and rarely have serious conflicts. Other similarities include their sense of caution (by similar joinings of the lines of head and life), strong life lines (revealing good health and physical vitality), lines of intuition, and clear lines of Apollo, which show a love of beauty and creative ability. Both men have strong union lines and numerous travel lines, as they make frequent trips.

In addition to their love for each other, they genuinely enjoy each other's company, whether at work, home or travel. While they have a wide circle of friends, they are very much a couple and are seen as a 'model' for their friends and acquaintances.

ANALYSIS 3 (Figure 12.5)

These are the hand prints of a 4-year-old boy. Even at this early age, there are strong indicators of temperament and his psychosexual personality. As the subject is right-handed, the separation of the head and life lines on the right hand (they are joined on the left) indicates that he is more self-confident than the earlier tendencies revealed (his parents describe him as 'fearless').

The 'mental' heart line is deep and long. It is also somewhat chained. This type of heart line reveals a sensitive and passionate individual, who can fall in love easily and remain very devoted to his partner. The samaritan lines would strengthen this caring nature. The heart line, however, is balanced by a

Figure 12.5: Analysis 3 – A
4-year-old boy

strong, realistic head line and a squarish hand shape, indicating a practical approach to life. The mount of Venus is large and well-formed, and reveals his high energy level. The thumb on the right hand normally opens as widely as that on the left, revealing independence and an unconventional way of seeing the world. The Mercury finger is prominent, and while not overly long, reveals good communicative ability.

At the present time, he has two clear lines of union in his hand, although they can barely be seen in the print. The hand prints of children can change dramatically in a short time, so it is a good idea to take follow-up prints of children's hands every year or so.

ANALYSIS 4 (Figure 12.6)

The hand of a 32-year-old cameraman and video engineer. Of all the people whose hand prints are reproduced in this book, this man's sexual history is perhaps the most unusual. Bisexual and involved with sado-masochism with both women and men, he has been sexually active since childhood. Over the years, he has participated in a wide variety of sexual practices with an equally wide range of people, including army generals and militant lesbians. He has also had sex with numerous farm animals. A motorcycle enthusiast, he claims to have enjoyed sex with a passenger while driving a motorcycle. At the time this print was taken, he was involved in a serious monogamous live-in relationship with a woman, who shares his interest in sado-masochism. This relationship can probably be seen in the strong union line on his mount of Mercury.

The low-set angle of the thumb and the wide space between the lines of life and head are two major indicators of his uninhibited sexual lifestyle and his unconventional views on sex and relationship. The large and prominent mount of Venus reveals strong passion and an abundant sex drive. The slightly short Jupiter finger may reveal a lack of self-esteem and hence the desire to prove himself sexually although it is neither obviously short nor weak.

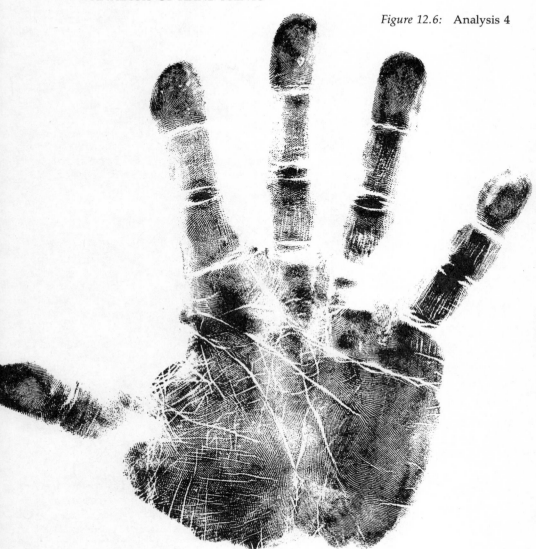

The subject has sometimes considered himself a sexual therapist of sorts (as seen by the samaritan lines on his mount of Mercury) and speaks about his sexual experiences with people (such as lesbians) who would not normally agree to have sex with a man. Here, too, there may be an element of trying to prove himself, but this is probably due more to his innate love of adventure and risk, as seen by the horizontal line moving from the percussion of the hand through the mount of Luna.

The head line is basically clear and strong, revealing a clear mind and good intelligence. The heart line is long and sensitive, with the downward branch revealing the potential for conflicts between the mind and the emotions in matters of relationship. The chained heart line acts as a balance for the somewhat coarse skin texture of the hand. His long, straight Mercury finger reveals good communication skills and an honest, straightforward way of dealing with others.

ANALYSIS 5 (Figure 12.7)

The hand of a 37-year-old actress/comedienne, who is also an excellent palmist. The keywords one can use to describe her hand can be pleasure-loving and spontaneous. She enjoys sex very much, and it is often the major theme of her comedy skits.

Her strong physical heart line would reveal an interest in intense and exciting sexual scenes, and the separation between the lines of life and head reveal her impulsiveness, impatience and lack of sexual inhibition. Her prominent mount of Venus, as well as her soft, fleshy hand and fingers, reveal her love of pleasure, which often includes food (she claims that the only French words she knows are 'soupe du jour'). The short, smooth fingers reveal a spontaneous, instinctual person who has little time for analysis and detail.

The subject has a straight and strong Mercury finger, which favours good communication and an honest and direct way in dealing with people. Her numerous healing lines can indicate her interest in helping others through palmistry, and her large mount of Luna betrays a protective and nurturing 'Earth Mother' type of personality. The long Jupiter finger indicates her tendency to be domineering and have things 'her own way'. The numerous lines in the hand reveal a highly sensitive person, while the diagonal lines moving up the mount of Luna reflect her psychic ability.

At the time this print was taken, she had been

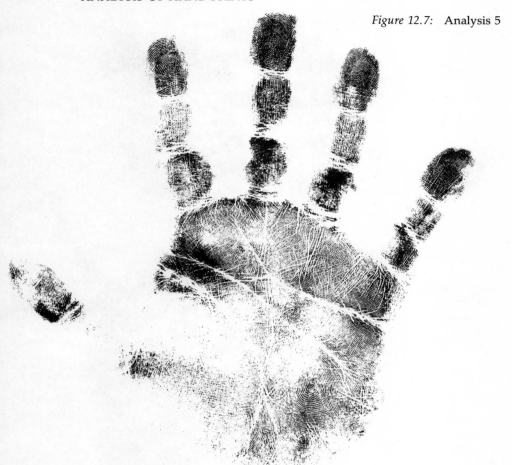

Figure 12.7: Analysis 5

married for two years and her rather weak union line was beginning to grow. She is very much in love with her husband and is committed to her relationship with him and their new child.

ANALYSIS 6 (Figure 12.8)

The hand of a 25-year-old man. The major reason for including this print here is that the individual is a virgin and has never had a romantic attachment in his life.

While some people choose to remain celibate until

149

Figure 12.8: Analysis 6

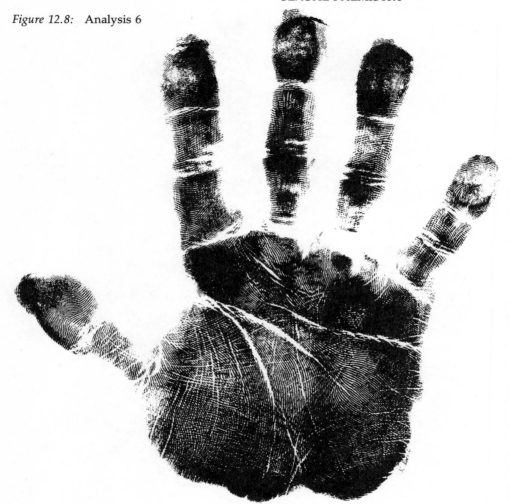

they meet their mate, the primary reason for this person's inexperience is sexual inhibition.

The subject has a good mount of Venus (indicating vitality and sexual energy) and a strong mount of Luna, revealing a protective nature towards others and strong instincts. The Mercury finger is of satisfactory length and size, revealing an ability to communicate well with others.

There are several indicators on the hand which

150

can reveal potential difficulties in relationship. The two drooping union lines early in life are often found on people who are perennially single, and who often place their careers before all else. The long joining of the lines of head and life indicate extreme caution, a lack of self-confidence, possible sexual repression and a fear of 'what others may think'. The islanded head line (especially before 30 years of age) reveals emotional problems, confusion and lack of focus. The heart line is sensitive and mental, yet it ends under the Saturn mount, revealing that the subject is ruled more by his mind than his feelings. At the same time, the girdle of Venus adds to his sensitive, romantic nature, and strengthens sexual feelings. The space between the heart and head lines is narrow, revealing a secretive nature and a tendency to repress his feelings. It is obvious that such contradictory elements in the hand can produce major difficulties both within the subject and in his relationships with others.

However, a prominent union line appearing further up the hand may indicate that a romantic attachment may take place in the future. However, much will depend on how the individual works to resolve the issues of lack of self-worth, fear, and the tendency to repress his feelings.

ANALYSIS 7 (Figure 12.9)

The hand-print of a 90-year-old man. A former logger and construction worker, he married early in life and fathered nine children. After his wife died, he eventually remarried, at the age of 77, to an attractive woman several years younger than himself, who had also lost her mate some years before.

The outstanding feature of his hand are the spatulate fingers, revealing a dynamic, adventurous individual with a strong sensuous nature. The clear and well-defined lines (especially those of life, head and heart) add to his physical energy, which also perhaps made him appear far younger than his years. His large mount of Venus would reflect that he was sexually active until his late 80s at least. A strict vegetarian and an avid gardener, he was physically active until just two months before his death at the age of 91.

Figure 12.9: Analysis 7

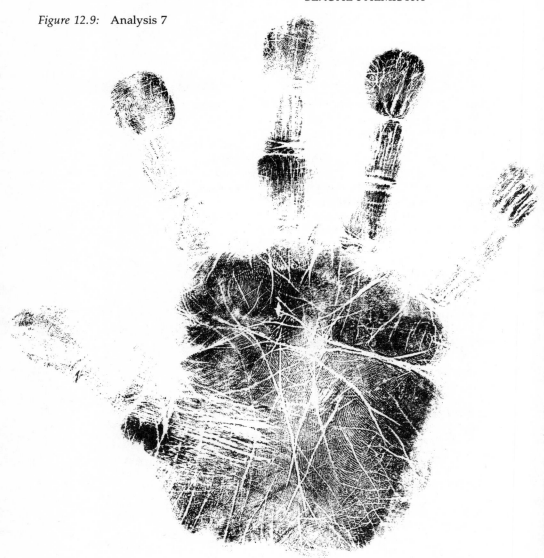

His strong mount of Venus, long Mercury finger, deep heart line and spatulate fingers reveal a man who enjoyed sharing love and affection. His wife often commented that he was 'the dessert of my life'.

BIBLIOGRAPHY

Aivenov, Omraam Mikhaël, *Love and Sexuality* (Frejus: Editions Prosveta, 1976).

Aivenov, Omraam Mikhaël, *Sexual Force or the Winged Dragon* (Frejus: Editions Prosveta, 1982).

Altman, Nathaniel, *The Palmistry Workbook* (Wellingborough: Aquarian Press, 1984).

Armstrong, Louise, *Kiss Daddy Goodnight: A Speakout on Incest* (New York: Hawthorn Books, 1978).

Arroyo, Stephen, *Astrology, Psychology and the Four Elements* (Davis, CA: CRCS Publications, 1975).

Assagioli, Roberto *Psychosynthesis* (New York: Penguin Books, 1976).

Bailey, Alice A., *A Compilation of Sex* (New York: Lucis Publishing Co., 1980).

Banerji, Sudhakar, *Palmistry, Sex and Marriage* (New Delhi: Sagar Publications, 1962).

Bell, Robert R., *Worlds of Friendship* (London: Sage Publications, 1981).

Bennett, J.C., *Sex* (York Beach, ME: Samuel Weiser, 1981).

Brenner, Elizabeth, *Hand In Hand* (Millbrae, CA: Celestial Arts, 1981).

Califia, Pat, *Sapphistry – The Book of Lesbian Sexuality*, (Tallahassee, FL: Naiad Press, 1980).

Churchill, Wainwright, *Homosexual Behavior Among Males*, (Englewood Cliffs, NJ: Prentice Hall, 1971).

Cook, Mark and Wilson, Glenn, eds., *Love and Attraction*, (London: Pergamon Press, 1977).

Evola, Julius, *The Metaphysics of Sex* (New York: Inner Traditions International, 1983).

Eysenck, H.J. and Wilson, Glenn, *The Psychology of Sex*, (London: New English Library, 1979).

Fitzherbert, Andrew, 'Spaces Between the Fingers', *Palmistry International*, Vol. 2, No. 3, pp. 81–3.

Fitzherbert, Andrew 'The Attachment Lines', *Palmistry International*, Vol. 2, No. 4, pp. 97–100.

Foote, Edward B., *Dr Foote's New Book on Health and Disease, With Recipes, Including Sexology* (New York: Murray Hill Publishing Co, 1903).

Fortune, Dion, *The Esoteric Philosophy of Love and Marriage* (London: Aquarian Press, 1967).

Fromm, Erich, *The Anatomy of Human Destructiveness* (New York: Holt, Rinehart & Winston, 1973).

Goldberg, Herb, *The Hazard of Being Male* (New York: Signet Books, 1977).

Haeberle, Erwin J., *The Sex Atlas*, (New York: Continuum Publishing, 1983).

Haich, Elizabeth, *Sexual Energy and Yoga* (New York: Aurora Press, 1983).

Hoff, John L., 'Practical Friendship', *In Context*, Summer 1985.

Holtzman, Arnold, *Applied Handreading* (Toronto: Greenwood Chase Press, 1983).

Janus, Sam *et al.*, *A Sexual Profile of Men in Power* (Englewood Cliffs, NJ: Prentice Hall, 1977).

Keleman, Stanley, *The Human Ground: Sexuality, Self and Survival* (Berkeley, CA: Center Press, 1975).

Klamkin, Marian, *Hands to Work* (New York: Dodd, Mead & Co., 1972).

Lasswell, Marcia and Lobsenz, Norman M., *Styles of Loving*, (New York: Ballantine Books, 1981).

Lee, Linda and Charlton, James, *The Hand Book* (Englewood Cliffs, NJ: Prentice Hall, 1980).

Leonard, George, *The End of Sex* (New York: Bantam Books, 1981).

Lewis, Samuel L., *Talks of an American Sufi* (San Francisco: Sufi Islamia/Prophesy Publications, 1981).

Lowen, Alexander, *Love and Orgasm* (New York: Collier Books, 1975).

Lowen, Alexander, *Pleasure* (New York: Penguin Books, 1975).

Luxon, Bettina and Goolden, Jill, *Your Hand* (New York: Harmony Books, 1984).

Mains, Geoff, *Urban Aboriginals* (San Francisco: Gay Sunshine Press, 1984).

Moore, John, *Sexuality Spirituality* (Tisbury: Element Books, 1980).

Morris, Desmond, *Intimate Behaviour* (Toronto: Bantam Books, 1973).

Nesfield-Cookson, Bernard, *Rudolf Steiner's Vision of Love* (Wellingborough: Aquarian Press, 1983).

Offit, Avodah K., *The Sexual Self* (New York: Congdon & Weed, 1983).

Pierrakos, Eva, *The Forces of Love, Eros and Sex* (New York: Center for the Living Force, 1978).

Pierrakos, Eva, *The Spiritual Symbolism and Significance of Sexuality* (New York: Center for the Living Force, 1973).

Pierrakos, John C., *Aggressive Functions in the Upper Half of the Body* (New York: Institute for the New Age, 1975).

Reich, Wilhelm, *The Bioelectrical Investigation of Sexuality and Anxiety* (New York: Farrar, Strauss & Giroux, 1982).

Reich, Wilhelm, *The Sexual Revolution* (New York: Farrar, Strauss and Giroux, 1974).

Rosenberg, Jack Lee and Rand, Marjorie L., *Body, Self and Soul: Sustaining Integration* (Atlanta: Humanics Limited, 1985).

Samois, ed., *Coming to Power*, 2nd ed (Boston: Alyson Publications Inc., 1982).

Singer, June, *Energies of Love* (Garden City, NY: Anchor Press/Doubleday, 1983).

Sorell, Walter, *The Story of the Human Hand* (Indianapolis: Bobbs-Merrill, 1967).

Spier, Julius, *The Hands of Children* (London: Routledge & Keagan Paul, 1955).

Thibodeau, Robert, *The Astrology of Love and Sex* (Ferndale MI: Mayflower Bookshop, 1982).

Weinberg, Thomas and Levi Kamel, G.W., eds., *S and M, Studies in Sadomasochism* (Buffalo: Prometheus Books, 1983).

Weingarten, Henry, *The Principles of Synastry* (New York: ASI Publishers Inc., 1978).

West, D.J., *Homosexuality* (London: Gerald Duckworth, 1955).

Wolff, Charlotte, *The Hand in Psychological Diagnosis* (New York: Philosophical Library Inc., 1952).

Wolff, Charlotte, *Bisexuality: A Study* (London: Quartet Books, 1977).

INDEX